Remembrances
and
Celebrations

Remembrances and Celebrations

A BOOK OF EULOGIES, ELEGIES, LETTERS, AND EPITAPHS

Edited by Jill Werman Harris

PANTHEON BOOKS   NEW YORK

The permissions acknowledgments are to be found on pages
302–308.

Library of Congress Cataloging-in-Publication Data

Remembrances and celebrations : a book of eulogies, elegies,
letters, and epitaphs / edited by Jill Werman Harris.
            p.   cm.
        ISBN 0-375-40123-7
    1. Eulogies.   2. Elegies.   3. Obituaries.
4. Bereavement.   5. Biography.   I. Harris, Jill Werman.
        CT105.H69   1999
    920.02—dc21   98-32149
                        CIP

Random House Web Address: www.randomhouse.com

Book design by Maura Fadden Rosenthal/Mspace

Printed in the United States of America
First Edition
        2   4   6   8   9   7   5   3   1

For Lloyd,
*in recognition of all that his interest
and support have meant.*

———————

AS. SOONE. AS. WEE. TO. BEE. BEGVNNE:
WE. DID. BEGINNE. TO. BE. VNDONE.

English memento mori medal, c.1650

CONTENTS

II. Letters   149

III. Elegies 231

INTRODUCTION

DEATH HAS BEEN marked and commemorated in every culture we know of since the beginning of time. "I know of no people for whom the fact of death is not critical, and who leave no ritual by which to deal with it," commented anthropologist Margaret Mead. The diversity of memorial rites is indeed a measure of the universal import of both the meaning of death and the significance of loss. But whether the practices are based on cultural, religious, ethnic, or completely individual beliefs, there is a common chord, which sounds again and again, and that is the powerful, primitive need to honor those who have died.

Historically, mourners have honored their dead with the ancient and persistent image of a death that wears two faces—the angelic and charitable spirit that will return to guide and protect them or the ominous specter that will rise spookily from the grave as some sort of contagion or incarnation of evil. Generally, mourners pay tribute with the hope of providing the deceased with a dignified exit from this world and easing the passage of the soul into the next. A meaningful and graceful farewell simply celebrates the person that was. But most significantly, the profound emotional, even moral, obligation to honor the dead provides great comfort to the bereaved, helping mourners in what poet Elizabeth Bishop wisely called "the art of losing." We cannot give those in mourning that which they want most—to have the dead back. But the act of honoring is itself consolatory: "Blessed are they that mourn," says the Bible, "for they shall be comforted."

For this volume I have chosen four channels through which we have historically honored those we have lost: eulogies; letters relating to death; elegiac poetry; and epitaphs. Reversing the common observation that there is a loss of words when confronting death, I present this anthology as an appreciation of the beauty and solace offered by words of loss. Shakespeare said, "Give sorrow words. The grief that does not speak whispers the o'er-fraught heart, and bids it break." *Remembrances and Celebrations* draws upon the vast literature through which people of all times and places have expressed sorrow, consolation, and importantly, gratitude. It is born of the powerful truth that if we are willing to love, we must also be willing to grieve.

I. Eulogies

Eulogies are an important aspect of the honoring ritual, one that is deeply embedded in the funeral tradition. Historically, a chief mourner lamented over the body of the dead and then eulogized the deceased, bidding farewell and offering prayers for the welfare of the departed soul by "paying of the divine honors." In a mythological sense, the act of eulogizing is worshipping the dead—a ceremonial parting of those of the earth and those beyond. More generally, eulogies bring the bereaved together, offering solace, and often courage, to mourners by remembering the individual life led.

When death strikes, few people have the ability to express themselves well, and often the bereaved are simply too dazed by grief to express themselves at all. Generally those who eulogize simply fulfill what is proper or socially prescribed, without truly doing justice to the distinct allure of the individual who has died.

A great eulogist honors the dead uniquely, speaking not only about what everyone treasured most but about what captivated him personally. Outstanding tributes illuminate the idiosyncratic essence of an individual and etch the spirit of the deceased upon our minds so that the person remains with us even in death. Over time the memory will dim, but the powerful bond remains unbroken.

Eulogies are a consolatory art, offering the interpretation and emotional support that a profound crisis often requires. They comfort the bereaved and are enormously cathartic for the eulogist, providing an opportunity to release the powerful emotions brought on by the death of a loved one. As Longfellow wrote, "The friends who leave us do not feel the sorrow of parting, as we feel it, who must stay, lamenting day by day." By remembering the dead, that sorrow is somehow transformed, the anguish transcended if only momentarily.

The eulogies collected here range from poignant to funny, but all are impassioned articulations, moving and often intimate portraits of family and friends. Some express profound optimism in the face of great sadness, others sheer devastation. But always they remind us how rich, full, meaningful, and good one life can be. As delivering a eulogy is also a self-defining act, we learn something rare as well about the individuals who gave these memorable farewells. It is my hope that the many selections in this book will enable ordinary people, not just writers and natural orators, to give eulogies that are affecting and meaningful.

For the most part, the eulogies in this volume were written in the twentieth century. On the whole, earlier funeral orations tend to be monotonous, unimaginative and, from my perspective, essentially without charm. Formal solace does not appear to fill the deep need for celebrating true individual virtues, as mourners routinely complained that the eulogies bore scant resemblance to the person being eulogized. Often they seemed designed in the belief that sorrow should be experienced and gotten rid of, preferably quickly and quietly. But bereavement is not an illness to be isolated and cured all at once. Death may be sudden but grief takes time.

II. Letters

The second section of this volume is devoted to three specific types of correspondence: letters of condolence, letters of farewell on the eve of death, and letters of grief. Here we find remarkably intimate and emotional musings, which express some of the most heartfelt and philosophical thoughts on death and loss. For me, this section best illustrates the fact that grief itself is often the tribute.

Although my collection spans several ages, most are from the eighteenth and nineteenth centuries, a time sometimes referred to as the Golden Age of Letter Writing. Here are the private papers of some of the great poets, writers, and thinkers of their time.

Despite the cultural and social metamorphoses that have characterized the passing centuries, these letters reveal that much of the way in which we express sorrow, counsel, or consolation has remained unchanged. The earliest work in this volume is a letter of condolence written on the occasion of the death of Cicero's daughter, Tullia. When we prune back the thicket of syntax used in 45 B.C. we see the same consolation that we use today, urging fortitude during the time of mourning and offering the comfort that "There is no sorrow beyond the power of time." Abraham Lincoln's letter of condolence reminds the daughter of his dead friend that she is "sure to be happy again," and Lady Mary Wortley Montagu advises her bereft daughter, "Do not give way to melancholy."

I was particularly drawn to the deep emotional utterances of men mourning the loss of their young children. William Wordsworth, grieving the death of his son, writes, "I dare not say in what state of mind I am." Dickens faces the death of his infant daughter and Tennyson mourns the death of his stillborn son. When Emerson discovers "his boy is gone" his suffering is indeed overwhelming.

In the letters of farewell, we see great concern for those left behind. Before his execution Sir Walter Ralegh tells his wife to "Bless my poor boy." Explorer Robert Falcon Scott, knowing the end is near, begs his dearest friend to "be good to my wife and child." Margaret Fuller, with her mysterious sense that she will not make the voyage home, blesses those whom she fears she will never see again.

Finally there is comfort for the bereft in two enduring themes: that the soul of the departed survives beyond corporeal death, and that when death strikes, it is the will of God. Philosopher Marsilio Ficino explains in his letter of condolence to a friend that it is the soul itself we love and now that death has come to pass, "we see the soul no differently then than now." Upon the occasion of the death of his mother Mozart writes, "God has called her to himself . . . he gave and he can take away." John Donne offers his mother comfort in knowing that "Our most wise and blessed Saviour chooseth what way it pleaseth Him."

III. Elegies

Elegies are among the oldest and richest forms of poetry. Contrary to common thought, elegy and eulogy, although parallel and potentially indistinguishable by verse, are not the same. An elegy is a mournful lament or poem for the dead, while a eulogy, as we will see, can be humorous, passionate, factual, or otherwise, but not necessarily melancholy. This conception of the elegy remains intact within this volume, although I have added, for their devious appeal, illustrations of grim humor. The collection of poetry also veers, in part, away from the more general premise of honoring those we have lost by including a diverse selection of work dealing with the overall experience of death.

The poetry of mourning often offers a touch of comfort when words of another form fail. Through a phrase or symbol, poetry allows us to rethink the experience of grief and endure the vast range of emotions that accompany loss. Oftentimes there is sorrow and despair, anger, rage, even regret. Langston Hughes' "The Bitter River" is a sorrow song, which mourns the loss of two lynched boys while also elegizing the more general oppression of the African-American people. At the other extreme we find hope, relief, and ultimately, as in Longfellow's "Psalm of Life," sheer defiance of death. Poetry can voice the fear and bewilderment of death as well as the courage and faith that are so vital to facing it head on. James Michener's "L'Envoi," the last sonnet he wrote, expresses his curiosity about where death will take him—the musings of a man who has lived ninety years and is ready to explore the inescapable, his ship "set to sail to seas unknown."

From the bereaved we see with great regularity the eternal hope or fervent insistence that the dead come back to watch over, visit, or haunt us. In "The Going," an uncomprehending Thomas Hardy wonders why his loved one continues to turn up at the end of an alley, "where so often at dusk you used to be." In "Footsteps of Angels," Longfellow mourns the death of his wife and brother-in-law and speaks of "the forms of the departed," who "come visit me once more."

Through those in mourning we are also witness to the uncanny physical symptoms of bereavement. Death can leave us literally gasping with grief. In fact, the metaphor of dying of a broken heart is a very real and dreadful phenomenon. It is not uncommon to hear a mourner lament that a part of him has died along with the deceased. Once deprived of someone we love, we die a little ourselves, as only the living can do. In "For Annie," Edgar Allan Poe writes of "the sickness—the nausea—the pitiless pain." In "Grief," Norah Leney writes of "the lump that swells inside my throat."

IV. Epitaphs

Epitaphs or tombstone inscriptions are an important part of the honoring ritual as well. Ordinarily contrived after several weeks or months of grieving, they are generally the last formal way in which we commemorate the dead. Epigraphic fragments can be traced back to the Roman graves of the early centuries A.D. Around the fifth century they started to disappear only to reappear, almost exclusively in Latin, around the twelfth century. By the fifteenth century they were fairly commonplace, corresponding with an emerging new attitude—the desire to assert one's own identity in death.

In some cultures it was believed that within the tomb the dead "sleep." Monuments with epitaphs were designed as a kind of shrine to ghosts. Ultimately, however, epitaphs exist to honor and preserve the memory of the dead.

Various people composed epitaphs, from clergymen to family members, professional writers for hire, and sometimes the deceased themselves, who feared to leave their reputations to friends, or to truth. The earliest epitaphs bore only the name of the deceased, but as time passed they began to include the dates of birth and death, age at death, occupation, and occasionally the relationship to the person responsible for the burial. Some are minibiographies—the cemetery a spiritual who's who of ghosts. At various times throughout history epitaphs have been garrulous, chatting away about everything imaginable from fear of the devil, judgment day, the doctrines of original sin, and even the details of someone's horrid end. Commenting on this, one eighteenth-century writer wrote:

Friend, of your epitaph I'm grieved
So very much is said:
One half will never be believed
The other never read.

Not all epitaphs are commemorative inscriptions on memorial tablets. Many are written in jest as a prank by friends wishing one's final memory to be a few perverse words. Some are intended but never actually show up on gravestones. Many still are poems or lines of text, expressing grief for the dead or describing them in verse or prose.

It is not uncommon for epitaphs to forewarn or give advice. One of the most chilling verses of all time is this widely quoted epitaph:

> *Behold and see,*
> *As you pass by.*
> *Where you are now,*
> *So once was I.*
> *As I am now,*
> *So you shall be.*
> *Prepare for death,*
> *And follow me.*

Pronounced from the dead, it warns that the end is inevitable. This kind of dead-writer-to-live-reader conversation is a persistent tradition within epitaph literature.

Many gravestones display passionate expressions of love, grief, or faith. Benvenuto Cellini's sorrow over the loss of his son is unmistakable in this short epitaph:

> *Giovani Cellini, Benvenuto's only son,*
> *Lies here, remov'd by death in tender years.*
> *Ne'er have the Furies with their murderous shears*
> *From Pole to Pole more hopes destroyed in one.*

Another notable epitaph reminds us that if you can't say anything nice about the dead, don't say anything at all:

> *Here lyes*
> *Dame Mary Page*
> *Relict of Sir Gregory Page Bart.*
> *She departed this life*
> *March 4, 1728,*

in the 56th year of age.
In 67 months she was tap'dd 66 times. Had taken away 240
gallons of water, without ever repining at her case or ever
fearing the operation.

Finally, many epitaphs do not conform to the seriousness of the circumstances under which they were composed. Some are deliberately comic and some downright vindictive. Many are rife with word play, with someone named More being described, for example, as "No More." It's almost as if some epitaph writers believed that death is the last great practical joke. Still, for many the gravesite serves as the point of contact with those we have lost and epitaphs are often the final and longest-lasting record of the ways in which we honor the dead.

In the simple belief that grief is one the most difficult emotions we encounter, this book is in praise of those who write about the dead. It offers readers a collection of work as an inspiration and appreciation of a very special, often overlooked, genre of writing.

I. Eulogies

T. S. ELIOT
by Sir Rupert Hart-Davis

A decade before the American-born poet Thomas Stearns Eliot's (1888–1965) death, he arranged for his ashes to be buried at St. Michael's, the village church in East Coker, a community in Southwest England, where his ancestors had lived for centuries. Eliot visited the small town in 1937 and soon after wrote the poem "East Coker," with the telling first line, "In my beginning is my end."' Wrote the poet, "Home is where one starts from. As we grow older the World becomes stranger, the pattern more complicated of dead and living."

On September 26, 1965, on what would have been Eliot's seventy-seventh birthday, a memorial was held at St. Michael's in his honor. Sir Rupert Hart-Davis, the publisher and writer, who had been a dear friend, spoke at the unveiling of a plaque below which Eliot's remains are buried. Sir Rupert speaks tenderly of Eliot's relationship with his wife, Valerie, who was thirty-eight years her husband's junior. It is said that the marriage truly transformed the end of Eliot's life.

I do not propose to say much about his works. His poems, his plays, and his essays are all in print and can be got from any bookshop or library. There are at least two excellent long-playing records of him reading his own poems, so that you can hear his voice. Many books have been written about him and many more will be written in the future.

But it is not of the great poet and critic that I want to talk to you, but of the man who wrote those poems and that criticism, the warm, affectionate human being whom his many friends loved and will forever mourn. . . .

In appearance he was the opposite of the romantic idea of what a poet should look like, as exemplified by his lifelong friend Ezra Pound. No long hair, Byronic collars, or unusual clothes for him. He was always neatly and inconspicuously dressed—elegantly, and always suitably, for he had a great sense of fittingness and tradition—his lined face usually grave, almost solemn, but in private, laughter kept breaking through. When you were with him you knew for certain that he was a great man, even though you might not be able to explain exactly why. I suspect that it had something to do with his obvious goodness. A younger poet, W. H. Auden, wrote of him after his death: "To me the proof of a man's goodness is the effect he has upon others. So long as one was in Eliot's presence, one felt it was impossible to say or do anything base."

That remark is completely true, but to someone who did not know Eliot it might suggest a rather priggish or forbidding person, a spoilsport, whereas in fact he was one of the most amusing and entertaining companions you could imagine. He had a lovely sense of fun. He loved jokes of all kinds—in his younger days, even practical jokes—and was a superb teller of amusing stories, which were made all the funnier by his precise diction and deadpan expression.

He had a great love of cats, as you can see if you read his delightful book of light poems about them, *Old Possum's Book of Practical Cats*. Later he became very fond of Yorkshire terriers. One day when he was being driven somewhere, he and the chauffeur passed the time by discussing the merits of their respective dogs. Eventually the chauffeur thought that perhaps he had overpraised his own dog, and said, "But, sir, he isn't really what you'd call a consequential dog." Eliot always said that he must write *A Book of Consequential Dogs*, but alas, he never did. . . .

He was also humble, in a way that perhaps only the great can be humble. In "East Coker" he wrote:

The only wisdom we can hope to acquire
Is the wisdom of humility: humility is endless.

And he lived up to this belief. He could, and did, talk about himself, his past life, and his achievements with complete simplicity and humility, as though it had all happened to someone else.

He was mild and gentle, courteous and polite, but he could quickly be roused to passionate indignation and speech by injustice or bad manners. Once, when he had agreed to give evidence in a court of law on behalf of the London Library, he was so apprehensive that he couldn't sleep the night before, and began his evidence quietly and with hesitation. Then, luckily, one of the opposing counsel made a remark to which he took exception. His eyes flashed, and he spoke with vehemence and passion, until finally he had almost to be dragged from the witness box.

I knew him best during the last eight years of his life, the years of his blessed second marriage. Until then his personal life had been for the most part lonely and unhappy. And then, as he approached old age, he found the perfect peace, understanding, companionship, and happiness which he had despaired of ever knowing. Just to see him and his wife together, holding hands simply in a roomful of people, was a moving and heartening sight. He expressed some of his feelings in the beautiful poem called "A Dedication to My Wife," which is printed at the end of the latest edition of his *Collected Poems*. It is the only one of his poems that is wholly composed of love and joy and gratitude. For several years before his death the doctors had given him up, and they could explain his survival only by his immense will to live. And he wanted to live because he was so happy. . . .

. . . However ill or disinclined he might be feeling, he insisted on appearing or speaking or writing on behalf of causes or institutions in which he believed. The London Library was one of these, and there were many others. Once in America, when he had read some poems at a party for such a cause, and signed all the copies of his books that were brought up to him, his admirers would not be satisfied until he had autographed the labels on all the empty wine bottles, which the exhausted poet obligingly did.

In small matters, as in great, his kindness was absolute. He discovered that I enjoyed smoking corncob pipes, and told me that the best ones in the world were made in his birthplace, St. Louis. He promised to bring me some next time he went there, and this promise he fulfilled, not once but three times, carrying these tiresomely fragile parcels half across the world and triumphantly handing them over.

The last words of the poem "East Coker" are "In my end is my beginning." Now the end and the beginning are one, and as you pass this tablet on the wall, say a prayer, by all means, for the great poet it commemorates, but, above all, say a prayer for the great and good man whom we remember today, on his birthday, with joy, with gratitude, and with love.

W. H. AUDEN
by Stephen Spender

From virtually the first time his poems appeared in print, in 1930, Wystan Hugh Auden (1907–1973) was recognized as one of the most important artists of his generation. Known for his sleek and wry intelligence, Auden commented on subjects ranging from social manners to faith and politics. Along with his friends and fellow poets Stephen Spender, Cecil Day-Lewis, and Christopher Isherwood, he was part of his own Auden's Circle, a poetry club whose work was strongly influenced by the prose of their idol T. S. Eliot.

Auden was an intensely private man but later in his life publicly acknowledged his homosexuality. In 1934 he entered into an arranged marriage with Erika Mann, the daughter of writer Thomas Mann, expressly for Ms. Mann to gain British citizenship before the Nazis canceled her German residency.

In 1946 Auden, who was English-born, became an American citizen. But toward the end of his life, he returned to England, becoming Professor of Poetry at Oxford. He spent half of each year in Kirschstetten, Vienna, and it is there that he died at the age of sixty-six. When, on October 2, 1974, Auden's name was joined with the illustrious poets in Westminster Abbey's Poets' Corner, his dear friend Stephen Spender delivered this address in his honor.

Wystan Hugh Auden is received within these walls, *in diesen heiligen Hallen.* I am sure that to him this ceremony would seem Mozartian: like being transported into the music of *The Magic Flute*, of which he and his friend Chester Kallmann wrote their version of the libretto. . . .

As both man and poet, for him this would seem homecoming; or perhaps I should say going home. For Auden, like Herman Melville, whom he so much admired, was one of those who arrive home by a circuitous route. As a citizen, he considered himself a New Yorker; as a colleague, his first and last home was

Oxford: in early days among his fellow poets, Louis MacNeice, Cecil Day-Lewis, Rex Warner, and Sir John Betjeman, and towards the end of his life at the high table of Christ Church, his old college. As a poet whose first love, even before poetry, was music, the village of Kirchstetten near the Vienna of great composers was home. He is buried in Kirchstetten and another monument bears his name. But all these homes return to the England of the limestone Northern landscape of his childhood in the green and river-running countryside, which he always regarded as the Garden of Eden.

And his first and last home was the Church of England. He would feel the utmost fulfillment is being received within these sacred walls, the body of the English Church, for his religion was to him more important even than poetry or music. However, it is as a poet that his name is spelled out in the Poets' Corner, here in the centre of London, where the stones and skies are mostly grey and where the pigeons outside are like grey stones flying between grey walls. I mention birds designedly because Auden's feelings about home are made particularly vivid for me by an anecdote recorded by his friend Dr. Oliver Sacks, who recalls being with him in New York:

> Once we saw a bird fly to its nest atop a sooty lamp-post in St. Mark's Place: "Look!" exclaimed Wystan, "It's gone home to its nest. Think how cozy it must be in its nest!"

This anecdote brings Wystan idly to me. I see him turning to his companion with that clarifying entertained sideways glance which would accompany such a very exposed comment: "just think of him flying to his nest!"

And if the recollection glashes to you a somewhat grotesque vision of Auden appearing in the precincts of Westminster or Trafalgar Square in the likeness of a somewhat bulky pigeon, flying not without difficulty and perching on a lamp-post, that is just as it should be: with him the grotesque or absurd stands close to the appropriate and serious. The shocking, the outrageous had for him an awakening touch. The joking word pointed to the highest reality was the bait that drew poetry to it, and was incongruous with his religion.

When, as happened once within these sacred walls, he preached a sermon, he usually managed to smuggle into it at least one phrase which, if it had not been partly muffled by the ambiguities of his collided Oxford and New York vowels and consonants, might have stunned some of the more conventional members of his audience. They were perhaps fortunate on such occasions to be able to go away not believing that they had heard what he had only mumbled.

Although he himself, if he were here, might feel nothing but gratitude that his poetic fame had provided him with a passport which enabled his name to become so literally a part of the body of the Abbey, it is as a poet that we think of him today. We think of his name on the stone near to those of colleagues belonging to this company of poets before he was born and near to that of one who was his contemporary—T. S. Eliot, whom he and all our generation of slightly younger poets admired this side of idolatry.

I should like then to say something about the nature of that poetry which justifies us in honouring Auden as he is now honoured.

Auden did not attach to poetry the immense pretensions which fill many poets at once with a sense of their transcendent personal superiority and with a sense of the near-unattainability of their objective aims in their work. He thought of a poem as a verbal object made by a craftsman who was to be judged to a great extent, though not entirely, by his technical competence in shaping language. At the same time he knew well that the modern poet, by taking many untamed, seemingly unpoetic, and even abstruse complex objects and naming them in diverse poetic forms, could make them familiar, accessible, capable of being handled like stones or bits of wood, could also make them, on occasion, sacred objects . . . He broke down great areas of contemporary experience into objects controlled by wit, crackling in jokes or transformed into objects of terrifying beauty. . . .

... He had also the strongest sense that poets should be modest in their claims on truth, that they should not indulge in the rhetorical lies which come so easily even to the greatest poets. When, with his wisdom, sense of beauty, and wit he directed his gaze upon the centre of the stage of our modern world, he was able to portray us in our situation, in poetry that combines accuracy of analysed experience with an authority of the imagination that shows our world to us as it is, while contrasting it with a vision of a life based on acceptance of a humanity which, despite its limitations, can still retain a certain innocence of nature: a glimpse of that Garden of Eden which the poet had first found in the green landscape of the England of his childhood.

HILDA STEGNER
by Wallace Stegner

Wallace Stegner (1909–1993) was the author of such books as **Wolf Willow** *(1962),* **Crossing to Safety** *(1987),* **The Spectator Bird** *(1976), and* **Angle of Repose** *(1971). He was a quintessentially American master storyteller, who was appreciated for his subtle but wise style. He often wrote about love, hurt, abandonment, strength, and the overall chaos and contradiction of the human predicament. Stegner's realm was life in the Great Plains of North America, celebrating the prairie and the wilderness of his childhood. Serving on the boards of the Sierra Club and the Wilderness Society and establishing the Committee for Green Foothills, he spent a good deal of his adult life trying to educate the public about America's natural treasures. Long respected as a teacher, he developed and directed the creative writing program that bears his name at Stanford University. Stegner's mother, Hilda, died in 1934. Remembering the anniversary of her death, fifty-five years later, he wrote this letter in tribute to her.*

Mom, listen.

In three months I will be eighty years old, thirty years older than you were when you died, twenty years older than my father was when he died, fifty-seven years older than my brother was when he died. I got the genes and the luck. The rest of you have been gone a long time.

Except when I have to tie my shoelaces, I don't feel eighty years old. I, the sickly child, have outlasted you all. But if I don't feel decrepit, neither do I feel wise or confident. Age and experience have not made me a Nestor qualified to tell others how to live their lives. I feel more like Theodore Drieser, who confessed that he would depart from life more bewildered than he had arrived in it. Instead of being embittered, or stoical, or calm, or resigned, or any of the standard things that a long life might have made me, I confess that I am often simply lost, as much in need of comfort, understanding forgiveness, uncritical love— the things you used to give me—as I ever was at five, or ten, or fifteen.

Fifty-five years ago, sitting up with you after midnight while the nurse rested, I watched you take your last breath. A few minutes before you died you half raised your head and said, "Which . . . way?" I understood that: you were at a dark, unmarked crossing. Then a minute later you said, "You're a good . . . boy . . . Wallace," and died.

My name was the last word you spoke; your faith in me and love for me were your last thoughts. I could bear them no better than I could bear your death, and I went blindly out into the November darkness and walked for hours with my mind clenched like a fist.

I knew how far from true your last words were. There had been plenty of times when I had not been a good boy or a thoughtful one. I knew you could no longer see my face, that you spoke from a clouded, drugged dream, that I had already faded to a memory that you clung to even while you waned from life. I knew that it was love speaking, not you, that you had already gone, that your love lasted longer than you yourself did. And I had some dim awareness that as you went away you laid on me an immense and unavoidable obligation. I would never get over trying, however badly or sadly or confusedly, to be what you thought I was.

Obviously you did not die. Death is a convention, a certification to the end of pain, something for the vital-statistics book, not binding upon anyone but the keepers of graveyard records. For as I sit at the desk, trying to tell you something fifty-five years too late, I have a clear mental image of your pursed lips and your crinkling eyes, and I know that nothing I can say will persuade you that I was ever less than you thought me. Your kind of love, once given, is never lost. You are alive and luminous in my head. Except when I fail to listen, you will speak through me when I face some crisis of feeling or sympathy or consideration of others. You are a curb on my natural impatience and competitiveness and arrogance. When I have been less than myself, you make me ashamed even as you forgive me. You're a good . . . boy . . . Wallace. . . .

E. B. WHITE
by Peter De Vries

Elwyn Brooks White (1899–1985) studied under the great grammarian William Strunk, Jr., at Cornell University. When White updated and revised Strunk's 1918, privately printed **Elements of Style**, *it gained him a reputation as the supreme stylist of his time. But White was much more than that. He was a brilliant essayist, most notably at* **The New Yorker**, *where his sophisticated, irreverent, and funny stories did much to create the magazine's tone. He wrote one of the most adored children's books,* **Charlotte's Web**, *and was an accomplished humorist and poet.*

White, who never liked his given name, Elwyn, and was nicknamed Andy, married his wife, Katharine, in 1929. He later said, "I soon realized that I had made no mistake in my choice of a wife. I was helping her pack an overnight bag one afternoon when she said, 'Put in some tooth twine.' I knew then that a girl who called dental floss tooth twine was the girl for me." Katharine died in 1977.

Peter De Vries, best known as a comic novelist, was the author of twenty-five books. He was a contributor to **The New Yorker**, *an editor of* **Poetry** *magazine, and a dear friend of E. B. White's, upon whose death he paid this tribute.*

The subtleties of civilized intercourse exacting, as they often do, a measure of dissimulation, many of us in this context or that may offer to the world an exterior not always in strictest harmony with the private self. With E. B. White one had the feeling that any such variance between—to oversimplify—the personality and the character was at an absolute minimum, if not nonexistent. This very lack of complexity made him a phenomenon among expectedly intricate types. The facade was the edifice. What you got was what you saw, from earliest acquaintance through ripening friendship. What was it you got, then? A gentleman, in that pristine sense of the word best apprehended by mentally dividing it up into the two words it comprises. And imagine my being so acutely conscious of White the stylist and style authority that in writing the foregoing sentence I looked up the word "comprise" to make sure I was using it correctly and not in the often mistaken sense of "compose," all this in the certainty that I understand the distinction completely. The whole comprises the parts, not the parts the whole. Well, as a gentleman he might have smiled seeing me do this, but gently. He was that not only in his personal relations but even when engaged in literary contention. Every boxing referee states the principle in that ritual huddle with the combatants just before the fists begin to fly. Come out fighting, but no low blows, and break even in the clinches. Perfect English, not a wasted word.

Most of us when on the attack occasionally reach for the old meat axe, but for him the scalpel sufficed, because he wielded it with such persuasive dexterity, the precise language ever at the service of a clear mind. "Limpid as dammit," as the Wodehouse character so limpidly put it. American journalism never had anyone quite like him, though he shared one quality with an essayist he could not have been more unlike in other respects—H. L. Mencken. That trait was clarity. Mencken was also limpid as dammit. He stated the case for both of them when he said of himself, "There is never any doubt about what I mean." There was never any doubt about what White meant . . .

If, as the Oscar Wilde character says, a man cannot be too careful in his choice of enemies, White was not attending to his life at all. No gift for enmity here. No one ever met anyone who didn't like him personally, however many may have envied him his protean talents—humorist, short-story writer, essayist, author of some of our most enduring stories for children, even gag writer for cartoonists. We recall with pleasure his magazine cover showing a seahorse wearing a feedbag, certainly whimsicality at its freshest. And of course half a century of snappers for *The New Yorker* newsbreaks alone qualify him as one of the wits of our time. . . .

. . . [Harold] Ross founded *The New Yorker*, but two or three of his early luminaries helped him create it, chiefly White and

Thurber as the most stunning journalistic pair since Addison and Steele, together with Andy's beloved Katharine, with whom he came to share a marriage of true minds to which impediment can scarcely be imagined. The subject of marriage offers the eulogist an occasion to recall one of his own favorite pieces of White light verse, "Husbands and Wives":

> *Those that call each other Darling*
> *Spend a lot of time in quarreling.*
> *Those that call each other Hey*
> *Live in peace by night and day . . .*

Early on, he had—to pluck Eliot out of context for a moment—found "some way incomparably light and deft, some way we both should understand," which served him equally in dealing with casual and weighty matters. Becoming heavy-hearted never made him heavy-handed. What a river of gentle yet consistently trenchant belles-lettres. What delectable parodies, what funny stories. What finely honed humanitarian admonitions. What delightful poems. What a contribution to the gaiety of nations. . . .

He lived a long and full life, full enough, certainly to include his own share of that human staple, simple melancholy. He loved his fellow men and he loved his fellow creatures. I wouldn't know whether White ever prayed; he certainly attended no church. Well, he prayeth best who loveth best all things both great and small. I trust it's not too cryptic to say that he had too much natural reverence to need religion. Thoreau was his god, or one of them. And did our modest friend, I wonder, ever suspect what we all now seem quite sure of, that all those years he was worshipping an equal?

DASHIELL HAMMETT
by Lillian Hellman

Dashiell Hammett (1894–1961), the author of **The Maltese Falcon**, *was one of America's most memorable twentieth-century mystery writers. Hammett, a former Pinkerton operative, used his experience and attitude to create the memorable character Sam Spade, his tough and true-to-life investigator. Well-known for his strong public stance against McCarthyism, in 1951 Hammett refused to name names for the House Committee on Un-American Activities and was imprisoned for six months.*

Hammett was an admitted alcoholic whose difficulties were often expressed in his personal life. His thirty-year-long relationship with writer Lillian Hellman is a legendary literary entanglement, which was characterized by conflict and devotion. She was the model for Nora Charles, the cool and witty wife in his book **The Thin Man**. *He supported, encouraged, and edited her work but was terribly unfaithful. She was madly in love with him, admired him, and remained devoted to him in life and to his memory in death. They were two proud and independent people, and it is fortunate to include the eulogy that Hellman gave at his funeral. Hammett, who was a veteran of two wars (he volunteered for World War II even though he was in his late forties), wished to be buried in Arlington National Cemetery but his funeral was held in New York City at the Frank E. Campbell funeral home on Madison Avenue.*

A few weeks ago, on a night when he was having a tough time, I said, "You're a brave man." I had never said such a thing before, and as he came out of that half doze the very sick have from minute to minute, he smiled and said, "Better keep words like that for the end." The end has come and he would not have wanted words today. This small funeral, this small tribute, I arranged for my sake. He was a man who respected words in books and suspected them in life; he believed that words some-times took the place of thought and almost always took the place of action, and he deeply believed in both.

With very little school behind him, Dashiell Hammett had the greatest respect for knowledge of anybody I have ever known. He read enormously, sometimes five and six books a week, and anything that came to hand. There were the years when there were stacks of books on mathematics. And then on chess, teaching himself by memorizing the problems and mum-bling them to himself; there was a year when he was interested in the retina of the eye, and another year when he bought a hearing aid and wandered in the woods trying to find out of it would make the sounds of birds and animals come clearer. Poetry, fiction, science, philosophy—any book that came to hand. He believed in the salvation of knowledge and intelli-gence, and he tried to live it out.

I have asked myself many times in these last thirty years why he seemed to me a great man. Perhaps because the combina-tions in the nature were so unexpected and so interesting. He didn't always think well of people and yet I've never known anybody else who gave away anything he had to anybody who needed it, or even wanted it, who accepted everybody with tol-erance. He didn't, as you know, think well of the society we live in, and yet when it punished him he made no complaint against it and had no anger about the punishment. The night before he went to jail, he told me that no matter what anybody thought he had no political reason for the stand he took, that he had simply come to the conclusion that a man should keep his word.

He was sick the night he came out of jail and it took me years to find out that wandering around the Kentucky town from which he was to catch the plane back to New York, he had met a moonshiner who had been in jail with him and was walking the streets with his wife because he couldn't find work. Dash gave him all the money he had in his pocket and he arrived in New York sick because he had kept no money to eat with. Many people would do just that, but most of us would have talked about it.

Dash wrote about violence, but he had contempt for it and thus he had contempt for heroics. And yet he enlisted in the Second World War at the age of forty-eight because he was a patriotic man, very involved in America. He went through three basic training courses with men young enough to be his grandsons, and told me later that his major contribution to the war had been to sit in the Aleutians and convince the young that the lack of ladies didn't necessarily have anything to do with baldness or toothache.

He was a gay man, funny, witty. Most of his life was wide open and adventurous, and most of it he enjoyed. He learned and acted on what he learned. He believed in man's right to dignity and never in all the years did he play anybody's game but his own. "Anything for a buck" was his sneer at those who did. In the thirty years I knew him I never heard him tell a lie of any kind and that sometimes made me angry when I wasn't envying the courage it takes. He saw through other people's lies but he dismissed them with a kind of tolerant contempt. He was a man of simple honor and bravery. Blessed are they, I hope, who leave good work behind. And who leave behind a life that is so worthy of respect. Whoever runs the blessing department, may they have sense enough to bless a good man this last day he is on earth.

JOSEPH BRODSKY
by Andrei Bitov

Joseph Brodsky (1940–1996) was a persecuted and exiled Russian poet. Denounced by a Leningrad newspaper for his "anti-Soviet" poetry, he was often interrogated, twice put in a mental institution, harassed for being Jewish, and finally arrested on the charge of "parasitism." But his poetry was not political. Rather, it was in protest against the drabness of life and the extinguishing of spirit in the Soviet Union. After he served eighteen months in an Arctic labor camp, Brodsky's five-year sentence was commuted and he spent the next several years trying to get permission to leave the country. In 1972 he was issued a visa and expelled from Russia, leaving his parents behind. He settled in the United States, where his poems, plays, essays, and criticisms were widely published. In 1987 he won the Nobel Prize for literature.

*Brodsky, who had a heart condition and had been in frail health for many years, died on January 28 at the age of fifty-five. Distinguished Russian novelist Andrei Bitov, whose best-known work is **Pushkin House**, gave this tribute to his friend.*

The death of a poet is not a death of personality. Poets do not die. Administrative power—that embodiment of a craven world—showed him many kindnesses and granted him great honors. But with all that came the accusations of parasitism, exile to the West (a forced mutation), and the refusal of a visa home to bury his parents.

I fear the 28th day of the month for my own reasons; these days, I shrink from it. The 28th is when things happen. A month ago, on the 28th, I flew home from New York. I called Joseph the night before. He said he couldn't seem to grasp an opportunity when it was there. The flight was canceled. I called him again. "See," I said. "The fates are giving you a chance." As it turned out, it was a chance they were offering not him, but me.

We talked about illnesses and operations and energies, and about the why and how of writing. And he repeated something he had once written—for Akhmatova, I think it was: "The word is a commandment, a spell, a charm. The grand design. And it may save." Today, at dawn, I felt I saw him. It was as though angels or doctors were leaning over his body. "Let us proceed . . ." "But you see, I'd rather stay where I am. With him."

He had always longed to be a footballer or a pilot, but his heart objected, fearful of the task. So he became a poet. They wouldn't even admit him back to the city where he was born to bury his parents. But then, he wouldn't admit the city—in its entirety—into himself.

It was always the 28th day. Especially 28th January in St. Petersburg: Peter the Great died on the 28th; Pushkin died on the 28th; Dostoevsky died on the 28th; Blok completed *The Twelve* on the 28th, and burnt himself out writing it.

A poet doesn't die in death; he lives in the heart. Not the organ, the metaphor. His heart ceased to beat; it couldn't bear the burden. He had to make a choice: die with his own heart or live with the heart of another. Everything rested with the heart. He might have taken the heart of a black racing driver killed in a crash. But he couldn't decide. The angels did it for him. They opened the way home, with his family there, in sleep. He died, and his own heart with him. The hungriest of Russian parasites is no more. We have seen the passing of a great sportsman and traveler. St. Petersburg lost its poet. On the 28th . . . That was the day he came back to us.

AGATHA CHRISTIE
by William Collins

Agatha Mary Clarissa Christie (1891–1976) was a prolific writer of mystery stories, creator of the clever, eccentric, and charming Hercule (Monsieur) Poirot and the indomitable Miss Marple. She is considered one of the best detective story writers and is beyond doubt the most popular. Christie was married twice, first to Archibald Christie and then to English archaeologist Sir Max Mallowan, with whom she traveled on several trips to Iraq and Syria, developing some of her best-known works, including **Murder in Mesopotamia** *(1930),* **Death on the Nile** *(1937), and* **Appointment with Death** *(1938).*

Agatha Christie was buried at St. Mary's Church in the village of Cholsey, England. She had earlier chosen her own memorial music, Bach's Air in D from his Third Suite, and her epitaph, or as she wrote, "Put on my slate: Sleep after Toyle, Port after Stormie Seas. Ease after Warre, Death after Life, Doth greatly please." Dame Agatha also requested that she be buried with her wedding ring. Several months later the memorial service was held in London, with the music she had ordered and a reading of the Twenty-third Psalm. Her longtime publisher Sir William Collins gave the eulogy.

It is over fifty years since I first met Agatha, shortly after the publication of *The Murder of Roger Ackroyd* had made her famous. The blurb of her new detective novel gave away a vital clue, and my uncle sent me, young and innocent, to break the terrible news. I was received with the greatest kindness, but little did I think at the time that this was the beginning of a long and very special personal friendship with one of the most wonderful and modest people I have ever met.

By her bedside, Agatha kept her mother's copy of *The Imitation of Christ* by Thomas A. Kempis, and on the flyleaf under her name, Agatha Mallowan, she had written:

Who shall separate us from the love of Christ? Shall tribulation, or distress, or persecution, or famine, or nakedness, or peril, or sword? . . .

I am persuaded that neither death, nor life, nor angels, nor principalities, nor powers, nor things present, nor things to come, nor height, nor depth, nor any other creature, shall be able to separate us from the love of God, which is in Christ Jesus our Lord.

That loving and lovely passage thoughtfully extracted from a chapter in St. Paul's Epistle to the Romans was her last message and is a reflection of the gentle Christian spirit that resided within her.

It is in this way perhaps that she would wish to be remembered, in spite of her worldwide fame as an author whose legacy to us is something over eighty-five books, one for each year of her life. Incomparable master, so we may call her, of detective fiction, she has held spellbound a multitude of readers the world over, and to her embarrassment wherever she travelled, Agatha was likely to be hailed a living wonder, for there was never anyone more genuinely modest. Her philosophy is aptly expressed by a quotation which one evening towards the end of her life she selected for a boy of eleven at his request. It ran:

I have three treasures,
Guard them and keep them safe.
The first is love.
The second is never do too much.
The third is never be the first in the world.
Through love one has no fear.
Through not doing too much one has amplitude of reserve power.
Through not presuming to be the first in the world one can develop
*   one's talent and let it mature.*

To the end of her days she was totally unspoiled by her fame as a novelist and playwright. . . .

In her own genre of literary work we must accord her the title of genius although she herself would never have admitted to any deep-seated literary pretensions. But she possessed in supreme measure one mark of literary greatness, the art of telling a story and holding a reader in its thrall, mesmerised by the narrative. Her characters often lightly but always subtly sketched are alive when we overhear their conversation as we enter into the room, seated or standing with them. Agatha had an extraordinary faculty of picking up bits of conversation and throwing them into a dramatic and sometimes tortuous plot, which usually defied the reader's ability to unravel . . . its unexpected and brilliant end, whether guided by the cynical realism of Hercule Poirot or by the quiet and unobtrusive subtlety of that acutely observant old lady Miss Marple, never without a touch of humour.

The exciting signposts guided the narrative but deep down there was a strong and underlying sense of purpose. Agatha herself liked to think of her detective novels not merely as preoccupied with the solution of crime, but as the equivalent of the medieval morality play, concerned with the interplay of the forces of good and evil, wherein the bad man was always brought to book, often with a flourish of trumpets. . . . She had a gift also for apt and sometimes recondite quotation and showed an easy familiarity with the Scriptures as in the apocalyptic title of *The Pale Horse*, whose rider's name was Death, and Hades followed him. . . .

And that is the note on which we may end—her gentle loving care for the good in man, and in beasts, for she had a succession of beloved dogs never absent from her thoughts.

In the many hundreds of letters received since her death, those who have written from many distant parts of the globe have blended admiration in equal measure with love, for Agatha knew what true religion means. The world is better because she lived in it. What greater tribute could be paid to her gentle memory?

MAMMY CAROLINE BARR
by William Faulkner

In 1902 Caroline Barr (1840–1940), a former slave, began working as a housekeeper in the Mississippi home of Colonel John Faulkner, the grandfather of Pulitzer Prize–winning novelist William Faulkner. After the colonel's death, Mammy Callie, as she was called, continued to work for the Faulkner family, becoming a second mother to William and his brothers, Jack and Johncy. Mammy Callie was the boys' childhood storyteller, and years later Faulkner drew upon her tales for the characters in his work. Caroline Barr raised William Faulkner, worked for him, and died in his home several days after collapsing from a paralytic stroke. After Faulkner had delivered the eulogy at the funeral, he sent a copy to his editor at Random House and wrote, "This is what I said, and when I got it on paper afterward, it turned out to be pretty good prose." Later he erected a marker upon her grave, which read:

MAMMY

HER WHITE CHILDREN BLESS HER.

In a final honor to Caroline Barr's memory, Faulkner dedicated his 1942 book, **Go Down, Moses, and Other Stories,** *to her. He wrote:*

TO MAMMY

CAROLINE BARR

MISSISSIPPI

(1840–1940)

WHO WAS BORN IN SLAVERY AND WHO
GAVE TO MY FAMILY A FIDELITY WITHOUT
STINT OR CALCULATION OF RECOMPENSE
AND TO MY CHILDHOOD AN IMMEASURABLE
DEVOTION AND LOVE.

Caroline has known me all my life. It was my privilege to see her out of hers. After my father's death, to Mammy I came to represent the head of that family to which she had given a half-century of fidelity and devotion. But the relationship between us never became that of master and servant. She still remained one of my earliest recollections, not only as a person, but as a fount of authority over my conduct and of security for my physical welfare, and of active and constant affection and love. She was an active and constant precept for decent behavior. From her I learned to tell the truth, to refrain from waste, to be considerate of the weak, and respectful to age. I saw fidelity to a family which was not hers, devotion and love for people she had not borne.

She was born in bondage and with a dark skin and most of her early maturity was passed in a dark and tragic time for the land of her birth. She went through vicissitudes which she had not caused; she assumed cares and griefs which were not even her cares and griefs. She was paid wages for this, but pay is still just money. And she never received very much of that, so that she never laid up anything of this world's goods. Yet she accepted that too without cavil or calculation or complaint, so that by that very failure she earned the gratitude and affection of the family she had conferred the fidelity and devotion upon, and gained the grief and regret of the aliens who loved and lost her.

She was born and lived and served, and died and now is mourned; if there is a heaven, she has gone there.

ANAÏS NIN
by Henry Miller

The legendary relationship between writers and lovers Henry Miller and Anaïs Nin (1903–1977) produced letters that reflect nearly a ten-year liaison. When Nin met Miller she was living in France and married to Hugo Guiler. But the marriage was hardly conventional and she and Miller began a passionate love affair. "Spontaneity incarnate" is how Nin once described Miller. Miller paid homage to Nin in his book **A Luminous Being.**

Nin was a novelist but her literary reputation blossomed with the publication of her diaries, which she began writing when she was eleven as letters to her father, who had abandoned the family. Nin also wrote short stories and went on to become a cult figure for young writers, particularly women. Toward the end of her life she divided her time between New York, with Guiler, and Los Angeles, where her new young lover, Rupert Pole, lived. When she died at the age of seventy-three it was fitting that Miller, who had been such a major influence in her life, gave this tribute.

It is only once or so each century that our sorry sublunary world is graced by the passage of a spirit as rare and courageous as was that of Anaïs Nin. In the realm of literature, I can think of few feminine figures who could hold a candle to Anaïs for artistic inventiveness and sheer personal radiance. Among these I would surely include Sappho, Emily Dickinson, Marie Corelli, Anna Akhmatova, and possibly the still-youthful Erica Jong. But few others seem to me to have possessed that special combination of toughness and magic, of power and elegance, which Anaïs and her counterparts so rarely and so perfectly embodied, both as writers and as women.

In a recent letter, Lawrence Durrell wrote that Anaïs had taught in her life and writings that women must put a high price on themselves and demand the right to be free, but that in so doing they should not lose their femininity—for, as Durrell put it,

> . . . the whole civilized world of good values upon which our children will depend for their growth and mental well-being is precisely the work of the feminine element. And a world without real women in it to guide and nourish and inform its values will fall apart.

Of the many women I have known in the course of my life, few could come close to Anaïs in beauty and feminine grace. She was both an enchantress and an aristocrat, a tireless helper of those in need and a fiercely private person. But she was also a writer of undeniable genius. And for all these reasons put together she now is the possession of the whole world, as it were.

I have repeated often before that her *Diary* ranks among the genuinely great and genuinely life-enhancing works of literature of all time. Now that her childhood diaries have been translated from the French and are about to be published, it will become even more obvious to her readers—the ones who have eyes and ears, *bien entendu*—how impressive has been the achievement of this lonely child whose only weapons, in the face of an unusually cruel fate, were pen and paper and the ink *étoilique* in which she very early taught herself to dip her pen.

Those who have humanly—all-too-humanly—criticized the work of Anaïs Nin in recent years have tended to accuse her of dwelling too much on "private" concerns. The writer of one current article in a widely read ladies' magazine, for example, says that "Anaïs' apolitical nature was self-indulgent and escapist; her analyses of poverty, struggle, and political realities were romantic constructs useful to very few." Such charges have a familiar ring. They would have sounded familiar to Plotinus, Boehme, Swedenborg, William Blake, Berdiaev, the Balzac of *Seraphita*, the Rimbaud of *A Season in Hell*, whom Anaïs loved so much, as well as to Sappho and Emily Dickinson.

But who would deny that these figures have done more to

initiate the inevitable task of "changing life" (in Rimbaud's phrase) than all the ones with the "correct" analyses of poverty put together? Who would deny that the whole sorry lot of orthodox commentators on "political realities" have a much less vital message to offer us than these so-called otherworldly spirits? Anaïs Nin, to my mind, belongs in this "celestial" company. Like them, she continues to speak to us. Like them, she will live forever.

RUPERT BROOKE
by Winston Churchill

The poet Rupert Brooke (1887–1915) was the embodiment of a generation of young men who went to war between 1914 and 1918. They were gallant and patriotic and rushed to defend their country. But they were unused to war and too often made the ultimate sacrifice. Brooke died on board ship in the Aegean Sea on his way to fight at Gallipoli. He was only twenty-seven when he died and had had only a small book of his sonnets published during his lifetime. Although his poetry leaves an enduring and gruesome image of young men at war, it is filled with romantic and beautiful images of life itself. When he died, the London **Times** *published his obituary, which was followed by a valediction written by Winston Churchill, who was at that time the First Lord of the Admiralty.*

Rupert Brooke is dead. A telegram from the admiral at Lemnos tells us that this life has closed at the moment when it seemed to have reached its springtime. A voice had become audible, a note had been struck, more true, more thrilling, more able to do justice to the nobility of our youth in arms engaged in this present war than any other—more able to express their thoughts of self-surrender, and with a power to carry comfort to those who watch them so intently from afar. The voice has been swiftly stilled. Only the echoes and the memory remain; but they will linger.

During the last few months of his life, months of preparation in gallant comradeship and open air, the poet-soldier told with all the simple force of genius the sorrow of youth about to die, and the sure triumphant consolations of a sincere and valiant spirit. He expected to die; and he was willing to die for the dear England whose beauty and majesty he knew; and he advanced towards the brink in perfect serenity, with absolute conviction of the rightness in his country's cause and a heart devoid of hate for fellow-men.

The thoughts to which he gave expression in the very few incomparable war sonnets which he has left behind will be shared by many thousands of young men moving resolutely and blithely forward into this, the hardest, the cruelest, and the least-rewarded of all the wars that men have fought. They are a whole history and revelation of Rupert Brooke himself. Joyous, fearless, versatile, deeply instructed, with classic symmetry of mind and body, ruled by high undoubting purpose, he was all that one would wish England's noblest sons to be in days when no sacrifice but the most precious is acceptable, and the most precious is that which is most freely proffered.

RANDALL JARRELL
by Robert Lowell

*Randall Jarrell (1914–1965) was a poet, literary essayist, and gifted but feared poetry critic. His friend the poet Robert Lowell said, "Woe to the acquaintance who likes the wrong writer, the wrong poem by the right writer, or the wrong lines in the right poem!" Jarrell's first book, **Blood for a Stranger**, was published in 1942. That same year he joined the Army Air Corps as a control tower operator, an experience that would provide much of the material for his future works. When Jarrell was killed at the age of fifty in a car accident, Lowell, whom he had met in the 1930s, remembered him in this tribute.*

Randall Jarrell had his own peculiar and important excellence as a poet, and outdistanced all others in the things he could do well. His gifts, both by nature and by a lifetime of hard dedication and growth, were wit, pathos, and brilliance of intelligence. These qualities, dazzling in themselves, were often so well employed that he became, I think, the most heartbreaking American poet of his generation.

Most good poets are also good critics on occasion, but Jarrell was much more than this. He was a critic of genius, a poet-critic of genius at a time when, as he wrote, most criticism was "astonishingly graceless, joyless, humorless, long-winded, niggling, blinkered, methodical, self-important, cliché-ridden, prestige-obsessed, and almost autonomous."

He had a deadly hand for killing what he despised. He described a murky verbal poet as "writing poems that might have been written by a typewriter on a typewriter." The flashing reviews he wrote in his twenties are full of such witticisms and barbs, and hundreds more were tossed off in casual conversation, and never preserved, or even repeated. Speaking of a famous scholar, he said, "What can be more tedious than a man whose every sentence is a balanced epigram without wit, pro-

fundity, or taste?" He himself, though often fierce, was incapable of vulgarity, self-seeking, or meanness. He could be very
tender and gracious, but often he seemed tone-deaf to the
amenities and dishonesties that make human relations tolera-
ble. Both his likes and dislikes were a terror to everyone, that is
to everyone who either saw himself as important or wished to
see himself as important. Although he was almost without vices,
heads of colleges and English departments found his frankness
more unsettling and unpredictable than the drunken explosions
of some divine enfant terrible, such as Dylan Thomas. Usually
his wit was austerely pure, but sometimes he could jolt the more
cynical. Once we were looking at a furnished apartment that
one of our friends had just rented. It was overbearingly eccentric. Life-size clay lamps like flowerpots remodeled into Matisse
nudes by a spastic child. Paintings made from a palette of mud
by a blind painter. About the paintings Randall said, "ectoplasm
sprinkled with zinc." About the apartment, "All that's missing
are Mrs. X's illegitimate children in bottles of formaldehyde."
His first reviews were described as "symbolic murders," but
even then his most destructive judgments had a patient, intui-
tive, unworldly certainty. . . .

It all comes back to me now—the just-under thirty years of
our friendship, mostly meetings in transit, mostly in Greens-
boro, North Carolina, the South he loved and stayed with,
though no agrarian, but a radical liberal. Poor modern-minded
exile from the forests of Grimm, I see him unbearded, slightly
South American–looking, then later bearded, with a beard we at
first wished to reach out our hands to and pluck off, but which
later became him, like Walter Bagehot's, or some symbolist's in
France's *fin de siècle* Third Republic. Then unbearded again. I
see the bright, petty, pretty sacred objects he accumulated for
his joy and solace: Vermeer's red-hatted girl, the Piero and
Donatello reproductions, the photographs of his bruised, merciful heroes: Chekhov, Rilke, Marcel Proust. I see the white
sporting Mercedes-Benz, the ever better cut and more deliberately jaunty clothes, the television with its long afternoons of
professional football, those matches he thought miraculously

more graceful than college football . . . Randall had an uncanny clairvoyance for helping friends in subtle precarious moments—almost always as only he could help, with something written: critical sentences in a letter, or an unanticipated published book review. Twice or thrice, I think, he must have thrown me a lifeline. In his own life, he had much public acclaim and more private. The public, at least, fell cruelly short of what he deserved. Now that he is gone, I see clearly that the spark from heaven really struck and irradiated the lines and being of my dear old friend—his noble, difficult, and beautiful soul.

ANDREW GOODMAN
by Ralph Engelman

At the age of twenty, Andrew Goodman's (1943–1964) consciousness led him to take part in the Freedom Summer of 1964, a project that encouraged voter registration among African-Americans in the Deep South. When Andy and fellow civil rights workers Michael Schwerner and James Chaney learned about the burning of a Longdale, Mississippi, church, they felt compelled to investigate. On June 21, 1964, they drove to Longdale in a Ford station wagon that belonged to the Mississippi Civil Rights Movement, a car well-known to the Ku Klux Klan and its supporters. They arrived safely but the city was seething with hatred over the just-passed Civil Rights Bill. The three young men were on their way back to headquarters when they were arrested for "speeding and suspicion of arson." They were released later that night but were never seen alive again. The deputy who had arrested them along with eleven other men had surrounded the three boys, beat them, and murdered them. Andy was shot once in the heart.

In New York City Andy's funeral was held at the Ethical Culture Society. His father, Robert Goodman, spoke first. In part he said, "Throughout our history, countless Americans have died in the continuing struggle for equality. We shall continue to work for this goal and we fervently hope that Americans so engaged will be aided and protected in this noble mission." One of the most memorable eulogies was given by Ralph Engelman, Andy's best friend. Today, Engelman is the chairman of the department of journalism at Long Island University. He said, "I was in Michigan and read the news of Andy's disappearance in the **New York Times**. *It was a nightmare, a very painful experience. I flew back to New York and had dinner at his parents' apartment. The bodies hadn't been found yet but everyone knew they were dead. I had been to their home a thousand times before. But now Andy wasn't there. It was devastating. I will never forget him. I still remember Andy vividly."*

Although I was perhaps Andy's closest friend, I do not speak for Andy. He always spoke for himself. It was one of his finest qualities. I can only speak about Andy, and try to state a just tribute and farewell not only to a martyr but also to a best friend.

We are a generation which does not know of the Great Depression, the Spanish Civil War, and concentration camps, and World War II. And we live in an age which often uses euphemisms to obscure rather than describe human suffering, and which sometimes appears to know how to use the word idealism only in a sarcastic sense. Andy was one of those rare individuals—rare in any generation—who are not satisfied with the wisdom and success they more or less inherit but do not have to struggle to achieve themselves.

Andy's decision to go to Mississippi was the result of a simple ability to perceive and feel the reality of the social evil which pervades our society. And for Andy the step from conviction to action, made quietly but firmly, came naturally. On the eve of his departure for Oxford, Ohio, Andy not only was conscious of the danger which awaited him, but also spoke with equal concern about the special risk being taken by Mississippi Negroes who would remain when the summer project was over. This was characteristic of Andy.

In going to Mississippi, Andy risked not only death but dying in vain. Whether the most important and publicized domestic crisis since President Kennedy's assassination will quickly disappear from the public consciousness or whether it will become a small watershed in American history remains to be seen. But the significance Andy's sacrifice will assume in the years to come will be a sure barometer of the fate of the cause for which he gave his life.

Andy has retaught us an old truth: that although we live and die alone, our personal happiness and destinies are inextricably linked; that none of us is free unless all are free; that we must demand not only comfort but also justice; and that there will always exist those superior souls such as Andy to remind us of these truths.

When far from home, I first learned of Andy's disappearance, my first reaction was to tell everyone around me that I knew Andy and to describe him, as if by doing so I could translate into human reality a name in the *New York Times*, because, I thought at that moment, Andy does not belong to the news media and certainly not to history, but to me as a friend.

The friendship, the love, of two young men is a nonsentimental, elusive kind of thing, but it can cut very deep. There were a thousand little but important things that were ours alone, and a part of me died with Andy. One of the things I liked best about Andy was that when he was angry or ill at ease or happy, it was always beautifully obvious. I will miss forever that unique combination of good-naturedness, of an ability to laugh with abandon and that intense seriousness and introspection that was Andy. I will especially miss his laugh. Then there was an Andy I think none of us knew—or, rather, an Andy we were just beginning to get to know.

Why should a future exist for me and not for Andy? Am I turning away from Andy when I look to the future? No, I cannot experience only rage and despair, if only because I would thereby repudiate the very hope Andy embodied. Andy's life is above all the victory of a human being, and of two parents and a family, a school, and also a society. It was the most painful moment of my life when I left Andy's home and his parents after my first visit since his disappearance, yet we did not feel as if we had lost Andy completely.

"And then I heard the door," William Faulkner wrote, "and it was as if [he] had not been. No, not that; not *not been*, but rather no more *is*, since *was* remains always and forever, inexplicable and immune, which is its grief. That's what I mean: a dimension less, then a substance less, then the sound of a door and then, not *never been* but simply *no more is* since always and forever that *was* remains. . . ."

If I do not speak for Andy, I would like to address my final words to Andy.

Andy—the world will never seem exactly the same without you; I will cherish the moments we spent together, and you will always remain important to me. I will draw upon you in the future. Because you once existed, I will never be quite the same. Perhaps our nation will never quite be the same. For although, like a pebble thrown into a lake, you are no longer with us, we can never be sure where the ripples spreading over the water will end.

OGDEN NASH
by S. J. Perelman

Ogden Nash (1902–1971) started out as a romantic poet but decided "to laugh at myself before anyone laughed at me," and soon became a master of humorous poetry. He used unconventional rhymes for his witty and memorable craft, often changing the spelling of words to fit his point—"that parsley is gharsley." He was partial to limericks and examined and made fun of everything from animals to taxes. In a review that missed Nash's point entirely, the London **Times** *wrote, "Mr. Nash's verse would be improved if the author took more care with his rhymes."*

Writer and cartoonist, S. J. Perelman won an Academy Award for his screenplay of the movie **Around the World in Eighty Days.** *His collaborative effort along with Nash and Kurt Weill on* **One Touch of Venus** *was the smash hit of 1943 Broadway theater. Upon Nash's death Perelman remembered his good friend.*

It was on an autumn day in 1937, as I remember, that Fate, in the person of a Metro-Goldwyn-Mayer producer improbably named Fleet Mousejoy, decided to interweave my destiny with that of Ogden Nash. What Nash and I were doing at that moment in Hollywood, a place both of us detested, and at M-G-M, a studio nobody could possibly recall with nostalgia, may be clarified in a very few words: we were merely two of the thousands of mechanics toiling in the dream factories in that vanished epoch, and chance had thrown us together at the writers' table in that particular studio's commissary. We had a certain prior connection, to be sure, in that our published work had appeared in the same magazine, but this was our first real contact, and very soon, on discovering that we shared the same prejudices, we became good friends. It was rather bizarre, therefore, when we were separately bidden into Mr. Mousejoy's office one morning and formally introduced, despite our protestations that we knew each other. Mousejoy was the kind of satrap who refused to believe that anything existed unless he personally had arranged it. "Now, boys," he announced after we had exchanged stilted handshakes. "We here at M-G-M have acquired a very important property—a best-seller that's cost us a pile of dough—and I feel you two are the ideal fellows to collaborate on the screenplay." He opened a desk drawer, withdrew a book, and laid it reverently between us. Our heads collided as we bent forward to inspect it. "What do you say to that for an assignment?"

How to Win Friends and Influence People, I read off, mystified. "Um—yes, Dale Carnegie. But look, Mr. Mousejoy—"

"That title on a theater marquee," declared Mousejoy impressively, "is worth conservatively one million dollars. And with the cast I have in mind—Joan Crawford, Fanny Brice, and Mickey Rooney—it'll be the blockbuster of all time. We're going to write a new chapter in motion-picture history, my friends."

"Fabulous," Nash agreed, "but there's one little hitch, Mr. Mousejoy. There's no actual story. It's a book of inspirational essays—psychology for the layman kind of thing."

"Ach—who cares?" the producer said impatiently. "That's where you two come in. A pair of brilliant minds working together—how can you miss? Now, I have a few ideas that may be helpful. Mind you, they're only suggestions . . ."

Nash and I listened attentively to his maunderings, retired to one of the noisome lazarets we occupied, and devoted a couple of days of fruitless discussion to Carnegie's classic. The only idea we could dredge up was that the Misses Crawford and Brice were strip tease artistes domiciled at the Y.M.C.A., but we couldn't invent any excuse to implicate Mickey Rooney in such a locale, so we abandoned that hypothesis. We did discover while conferring, though, that we both venerated the Sherlock Holmes canon, and we began evolving an intricate quiz that seemed to have strong commercial possibilities. Incredibly enough, five weeks passed without any interference from

Mousejoy. He phoned once or twice to inquire benevolently how we were progressing, but assured us he wasn't prying—he wanted our creative powers to range free, to be given the widest latitude.

Then, one day out of the blue, he suddenly summoned us into his presence. Naturally, we were appalled, as we hadn't a word on paper or even the ghost of an idea, but miraculously he didn't even ask. He merely wanted to apologize. He was being called to New York for some high-level executive meeting, and consequently was forced to postpone our picture and transfer us to two other producers. His voice shook with genuine emotion as he predicted that some day, in the near-distant future, our triumvirate would again work together.

The day did come, but the trio he envisioned was different. Six years later, Nash and I collaborated on a Broadway musical, *One Touch of Venus,* for which Ogden also supplied lyrics for Kurt Weill's score. We hammered out the libretto in a room at the Harvard Club, word by word in pencil on those lined yellow pads he always favored. He was a scrupulous, deliberate worker, as all his verse attests; he abhorred the slapdash, the hackneyed turn of thought, the threadbare phrase. And insofar as work can be pleasurable, I can't imagine anybody with whom one could feel a closer rapport. His understanding was so quick, his mind so fanciful and allusive, that it enriched whatever it touched.

We went on to other projects in the theater afterward, and never lost the spirit of harmony and enjoyment we found in each other's company. When geography and circumstance separated us in later years, my reunion with him was a delight; I felt privileged that I knew anyone of such cultivated and subtle intelligence. That his poetry was so widely acclaimed and his audience so devoted never surprised me, for the man himself had all its qualities—wit, compassion, and the extraordinary ability to enchant his readers—in the highest degree. I am grateful to have known Ogden Nash, and only sorry that those who know him merely from the printed page cannot share my love.

KATHERINE ANNE PORTER
by Robert Penn Warren

Katherine Anne Porter (1890–1980) was an accomplished writer known for her short fiction. Her major works include **Flowering Judas** *(1930),* **Pale Horse, Pale Rider** *(1939), and* **Ship of Fools** *(1962), her best-selling novel, which was published when she was seventy-two years old. In 1966 her* **Collected Stories** *won the Pulitzer Prize for fiction. Porter was born in rural Texas but spent most of her adult life in exciting cities during their most memorable times; New York throughout the 1920s, Paris during the 1930s, and Washington, D.C., during World War II and the Kennedy and Johnson administrations. Porter was by all accounts a complex individual: a femme fatale who managed to embrace feminism. Upon her death, her friend, writer Robert Penn Warren, paid her this tribute.*

Katherine Anne Porter was born on May 15, 1890, in Indian Creek, Texas—a new, half-wild land to which her family, good Confederates, had fled to rebuild their fortunes after the collapse of their world. And here, in my mind, I always linger to think on one of the strangest paradoxes in this life of paradoxes: Daniel Boone's brother Jonathan was Katherine Anne Porter's great-great-grandfather. The tough bloodstream did not run dry in her delicate veins. For the graceful, witty, sensitive, charming, gifted, not quite diminutive lady was tough. She was tough enough to survive all sorts of poverty, misfortune, ill judgment, distress, risk for causes that she happened to deem worthy, pain, self-denial, and a grim self-imposed discipline to follow what she took to be her star. But she always seemed to rise above the most dire circumstances . . . Courage and gaiety survived all.

To many who knew Katherine Anne in later life, Indian Creek often seemed a strange oddity in her biography, a trick fate had played on her. But it may have been a heaven-sent oddity. Where else on earth could she have learned certain things she knew? Manners and decorum mixed with the habit of a man's wearing a pistol in his belt to church? . . .

Indian Creek did, indeed, come to seem anomalous, for she early fled from that world—fled from it to the romance of Mexico, revolutionary ardor, art, journalism, and even movie-acting. But as it turned out, for her a "fleeing" was only a way of possessing more deeply the thing fled from, and after years during which the Mexican experience had entered the stories of her first volume, *Flowering Judas*, the Old Order began to bloom in her imagination. Even so, in the first work to spring from this impulse, *Old Mortality*, one of her most magnificent fictions, the repossession dealt not only with nostalgia (nostalgia seen through humor) and sympathy, but with a deeply paradoxical account of characteristic good and evil of that period, a subtle parable of history, and the human being's perennial problem of placing oneself in history.

By this time, however, the author herself had long since been confirmed in her wanderings in the New Order, a wandering prefigured in the last sentence of *Old Mortality*, in the innocent and ignorant promise that Miranda makes to herself in repudiating the past. By the time of *Pale Horse, Pale Rider*, which in subject matter deals with Miranda's discovery of the horror of the New Order, Katherine Anne had long since discovered that promises—especially promises one makes oneself—are undependable. . . .

It is very easy to say that our subject lacked a sense of reality, that she could never accept the actualities of place and time and human nature—the sense that the world, and life, are a mixed bag. This—even if such mixture is the subject of her own great fictional achievement. Yes, there were outrage and anger at betrayals; at self-delusion; at hate passing as love and love as hate; at both misnamed . . .

Splendid cookery, laughter in comradeship, generosity to the young, an almost childish love of such embellishments of life as velvet and emeralds, flirtation alternating with a most fierce set of chin—these things we remember. My wife reminds me that a woman as attractive as Katherine Anne Porter to men, and as pleased to be so, does not often look kindly on other women, especially younger ones. But Katherine Anne's style was grander than that. She kept her heart and eyes open for friendship wherever it might be found.

This was part of her unvanquishable zest for life. It is this quality that could make her laughter so infectious, so vital, so unforgettable. It was most rarely a laughter of malice. I think that we might call it a laughter of the absurd—rooted in comradeship, love of human qualities worthy to be admired, or works of art that claimed her devotion, and in a courage to face all ironies. As an artist, it seems that the most obvious word to describe her, if one word will serve, is dedication. As a human being she was an unparalleled combination of fun and fury.

She died at ninety. And until close to the end she could turn on the old spark and sparkle, and make the word energy seem pale and wan.

DUKE ELLINGTON
by Stanley Dance

Musical legend Duke Ellington (1899–1974) was a composer and arranger who left behind a vast body of work, including the amazing "Solitude," "Sophisticated Lady," "I Got It Bad," "The Moochie," and "Mood Indigo." Although his creations were invariably blues and his style jazz, Ellington rejected the idea that his music could be categorized and was considered a true pioneer in extending jazz composition. He performed in diverse settings from the Cotton Club to Carnegie Hall to Westminster Abbey. His songs are a wonderful part of the American cultural heritage.

Ellington's funeral was held on Memorial Day, May 27, 1974, at New York City's Cathedral of St. John the Divine, where he had presided over his enormously successful Second Sacred Concert. The church and the streets around were filled as ten thousand people gathered to pay their respects. As Ellington's coffin was wheeled from the church, mourners—Count Basie, who was sitting in the first pew, among them—wept. Ella Fitzgerald sang "Solitude" and the funeral hymn "Just a Closer Walk with Thee." Ellington's son, Mercer, chose his father's dear friend of forty years and author of The World of Duke Ellington, Stanley Dance, to give the eulogy. Mercer recalled, "I wanted more than the usual platitudes and consolation for the bereaved, and I felt he knew what I wanted better than anyone else. . . ."

It is hard to do justice in words to a beloved friend, especially when the friend was a genius of the rarest kind. . . .

As a musician, he hated categories. He didn't want to be restricted, and although he mistrusted the word "jazz," his definition of it was "freedom of expression." If he wished to write an opera, or music for a ballet, or for the symphony, or for a Broadway musical, or for a movie, he didn't want to feel confined to the idiom in which he was the unchallenged, acknowledged master.

As with musical categories, so with people categories. Categories of class, race, color, creed, and money were obnoxious to him. He made his subtle, telling contributions to the civil rights struggle in musical statements—in "Jump for Joy" in 1941, in "The Deep South Suite" in 1946, and in "My People" in 1963. Long before black was officially beautiful—in 1928, to be precise—he had written "Black Beauty" and dedicated it to a great artist, Florence Mills. And with "Black, Brown and Beige" in 1943, he proudly delineated the black contribution to American history.

His scope constantly widened, and right up to the end he remained a creative force, his imagination stimulated by experience. There was much more he had to write, and would undoubtedly have written, but a miraculous aspect of his work is not merely the quality, but the quantity of it. Music was indeed his mistress. He worked hard, did not spare himself, and virtually died in harness. Only last fall, he set out on one of the most exhausting tours of his career. He premiered his Third Sacred Concert in Westminster Abbey for the United Nations, did one-nighters in all the European capitals, went to Abyssinia and Zambia for the State Department, and returned to London for a command performance before Queen Elizabeth. When people asked if he would ever retire, he used to reply scornfully, "Retire to what?"

His career cannot be described in a few minutes. Where would one start? With the composer, the bandleader, the pianist, the arranger, the author, the playwright, the painter? He was a jack of all trades, and master of all he turned his hand to. Or should one start with the complex human being—at once sophisticated, primitive, humorous, tolerant, positive, ironic, childlike (not childish), lion-like, shepherd-like, Christian . . . ? He was a natural aristocrat who never lost the common touch. He was the greatest innovator in his field, and yet paradoxically a conservative, one who built new things on the best of the old and disdained ephemeral fashion.

I certainly would never pretend that I wholly knew this wonderful man, although I spent much time in his company and enjoyed his trust. The two people who knew him best were his son, Mercer, and his sister, Ruth, and their loss is the greatest of all. Otherwise, his various associates and friends knew different aspects of him, but never, as they readily admit, the whole man.

Song titles say a good deal. "Mood Indigo," "Sophisticated Lady," "Caravan," "Solitude," "Don't Get Around Much Anymore," "I'm Beginning to See the Light," and "Satin Doll" are part of the fabric of twentieth-century life. But the popular song hits are only a small part of Duke Ellington's priceless legacy to mankind. His music will be interpreted by others, but never with the significance and tonal character given it by his own band and soloists, for whom it was written. In that respect, his records are the greatest of his gifts to us. Here one can enter a unique world, filled with his dreams, emotions, fantasies, and fascinating harmonies. He brought out qualities in his musicians they did not always know they possessed. He had the knack of making good musicians sound great, and great musicians sound the greatest. As the best arranger in the business, he was able to furnish them with superb backgrounds, and as one of the most inventive—and underrated—of pianists, he gave them inspiring accompaniment. He was, in fact, more of an inspiration than an influence, and though he made no claim to being a disciplinarian, he ruled his realm with wisdom. . . .

Withal, Duke Ellington knew that what some called genius was really the exercise of gifts which stemmed from God. These gifts were those his Maker favored . . . He proclaimed the message in his Sacred Concerts, grateful for an opportunity to acknowledge something of which he stood in awe, a power he considered above his human limitations. He firmly believed what the mother he worshipped also believed, that he had been blessed at birth. He reached out to people with his music and drew them to himself.

There must be many here who can testify to his assumption—conscious or unconscious—of a father's role. Those he befriended are legion. His sense of family embraced not only the members of his band throughout the years, but people from all walks of life whose paths crossed his. Wherever or whenever he could, he personally resolved for those about him problems involving doubts, anxieties, illness, or grief. Loyalty was the quality he greatly esteemed in others, and it was generously reciprocated by him.

It is Memorial Day, when those who died for the free world are properly remembered. Duke Ellington never lost faith in this country, and he served it well. His music will go on serving it for years to come.

PAUL ROBESON
by Paul Robeson, Jr.

Paul Robeson (1898–1976) is best remembered as a multitalented actor and concert artist, whose performance of "Ol' Man River" and stage role of Othello thrilled international audiences. He was a brilliant linguist, who combined his knowledge of Chinese, Hebrew, Russian, and Welsh with his unusually commanding voice. Robeson, the son of an escaped slave, studied law at Columbia University, but his interest in the stage prevailed over a legal career. He became a cultural icon and a role model for African-Americans. He was an outspoken critic of segregation and racial discrimination in the United States and was deeply concerned with class struggle throughout the world. Robeson fell from grace when he refused to sign a non-Communist oath, a move that prompted the State Department to revoke his passport. As a result, his performances were disrupted and his bookings eventually canceled.

When he died in 1976, his funeral was held at Mother A.M.E. Zion Church, in Harlem. It is not only one of the oldest black churches in America and the former parish of his brother, Reverend Benjamin Robeson, but was one of the few places where Robeson could perform when he was refused elsewhere. His son, Paul Robeson, Jr., author, lecturer, and translator, gave the eulogy.

I cannot speak today of the full measure of the family's personal grief and overwhelming sense of loss. There are no words for that. My father's immense power and great gentleness, his intense spiritual force and great intellect, his unbending courage and his deep compassion have left each one of us with special memories that will always sustain us, for each was touched by him in a special way.

To me, his son, he gave not only his love but also the freedom and encouragement to think my own thoughts, to follow my own inner convictions, to be my own man. To all of us he gave, by example, a set of standards to guide our own lives, each of us in our own way.

But I speak today not only because I loved him as a father. I loved him as a friend and as a great and gentle warrior with whom I worked and fought side by side. And so I come to speak of both the disappointments and the triumphs of Paul Robeson's last years—disappointment because illness forced him into complete retirement; triumph because he retired undefeated and unrepentant. He never regretted the stands he took, because almost forty years ago, in 1937, he made his basic choice. He said then: "The artist must elect to fight for freedom or for slavery. I have made my choice. I had no alternative."

He knew the price he would have to pay and he paid it, unbowed and unflinching. He knew that he might have to give his life, so he was not surprised that he lost his professional career. He was often called a Communist, but he always considered that name to be an honorable one.

Paul Robeson felt a deep responsibility to the people who loved him and to all those to whom he was a symbol. When he felt that he could no longer live up to their expectations, he chose to retire completely. When he could no longer raise his voice in song to inspire and to comfort, he chose silence— because Paul Robeson's views, his work, his artistry, his life, were all of one piece.

But there was also gratification in retirement. In my father's last public message in June 1974 he said:

> It has been most gratifying to me in retirement to observe that the new generation that has come along is vigorously outspoken for peace and liberation. . . . To all the young people, black and white, who are so passionately concerned with making a better world, and to all the old-timers who have been involved in that struggle, I say: Right on!

And there was the secure knowledge that his own people, who had protected him and nourished him during the days of the fiercest oppression against him, appreciated his sacrifice and respected his privacy.

The one person who did most to give my father some joy in his last years is my Aunt Marion. It is she who created a haven for him in Philadelphia and surrounded him with those close old friends who made him feel loved and at ease. And I will always remember what my father said about Aunt Marion: "The thought of Sis always brings an inner smile."

Many other Philadelphians, black and white, expressed their respect and admiration for my father. During my father's last illness, his personal doctor and the entire hospital staff cared for him as if he had been their own loved one. And the people from all walks of life wrote him letters of encouragement.

It is fitting that my father now comes home to Harlem and Mother Zion Church. Eighteen years ago he wrote:

> Not far away is the house where my Brother Ben lives: the parsonage of Mother A.M.E. Zion Church of which Ben—Reverend Benjamin C. Robeson—has been pastor for many years. My brother's love, which enfolds me, is a precious, living bond with the man, now forty years dead, who more than anyone else influenced my life—my father, Reverend William Drew Robeson. It is not just that Ben is my older brother, but he reminds me so much of Pop that his house seems to glow with the pervading spirit of that other Reverend Robeson, my wonderful, beloved father.

There are others here today, and some who have passed on, who were as close to my father as anyone in his family. There are people whose lives he enriched and who enriched his life in return. I reach out to them today to share with them the family's grief, for they will always be part of us.

My father's legacy belongs also to all those who decide to follow the principles by which he lived. It belongs to his own people and to other oppressed peoples everywhere. It belongs to those of us who knew him best and to the younger generation that will experience the joy of discovering him.

Yesterday, someone very dear to me was reading some poetry and was moved to write the following lines. They say a great deal about my father's legacy:

He is not mine,
I may give to him my love,
But not my thoughts
He passes by me,
But he does not pass from me
For although he was with me in some ways
and will stay with me in others,
He does not belong to me.

I may keep memories of him
but not his essence,
For that will pour forth tomorrow.

JAMES MICHENER
by William Livingston

James Michener (1907–1997) captivated readers when his first book, **Tales of the South Pacific***, was published in 1947 and awarded the Pulitzer Prize. Michener went on to write forty books, many of which concerned his extensive travels throughout the world. When he died at the age of ninety his funeral was held at the Westminster Presbyterian Church in Austin, Texas. A bronze bust in his likeness was draped with a lei, for he had a special affection for Hawaii and his signature greeting was "Aloha."*

Michener's eulogy was delivered by William Livingston, senior vice president of the University of Texas at Austin, who had been his friend since 1981 when the then governor of Texas tried to persuade Michener to undertake a book on the state. The university's facilities were made available to enable him to accomplish the task, and **Texas** *was written and well received. In 1982, Michener became a professor at the university and taught at the Texas Center for Writers, now known as the Michener Center for Writers. The university had wanted to change the name for many years but Michener insisted, "Don't do it while I'm alive."*

Today we mourn the loss of a writer, journalist, philanthropist, and citizen of the world. But more than that, we mourn the loss of our dear friend and neighbor, James Michener. . . . We are gathered here today at the Westminster Presbyterian Church to celebrate his life, acknowledge his death, and wish him Godspeed to his destination.

Jim Michener was born in 1907 into the most humble circumstances, but he responded to the world he encountered by building a life of achievement and of service. Service to his country, in the military and as an advisor to governments and presidents; service to higher education as a teacher, scholar, and benefactor; service to the arts as a collector, patron, and museum builder; and service to his many communities, where he always found a way to improve the lives of the people around him. And no community has more to be grateful to him for than the University of Texas at Austin.

Jim Michener spent the first years of his life in Doylestown, Pennsylvania, and the last years of his life in Austin, Texas, which he chose as his home and as his final resting place. In between he lived in many other places, lived many lives, and lived with many friends, who today form a kind of international extended family. That family includes world leaders and people of great distinction, but it also includes many young students and budding writers whom he urged to aim high and to soar higher, and from whom expressions of gratitude and mourning have been flowing over the past several days. Michener's early life left him with a profound desire to help others. He grew up a homeless waif in the home of a generous and gentle woman named Mabel Michener. "Mrs. Michener," he wrote, "made her living by taking in orphaned children for whom the social services of the time paid her a pittance, and doing other families' laundry for which she received even less." Young Jim usually shared this home, furnished with little more than what he called "abundant love," with four or five other children.

He wrote about his childhood in his memoir called *The World Is My Home*. "I never had a wagon," he said,

> or a pair of roller skates, or a baseball glove, or a bicycle. One bleak Christmas a gentle-hearted woman who barely knew me summoned me to her home to give me the only present she could afford, a slim cardboard box with a flat lid containing a sheaf of worn-out carbon paper. She showed me how to use this magical stuff, and I spent all that Christmas enraptured with the idea that a person could write a sentence and have it duplicated endlessly.

Since then Michener has found a way to write many sentences and have them reproduced endlessly in ways that he could not then have imagined.

He had the imagination to find magic and rapture in that used carbon paper. And later he pursued magic and rapture in other ways. He exalted ideas and possibilities and he did it while pursuing his far-ranging interests all across the globe—his only navigator being his own curiosity. And his memory! By heaven, he never forgot anything he was interested in, and he was interested in everything. So what are we to say of him today? How are we to select from among all the things he was and did?

First and foremost, James Michener was a writer—a professional writer. He did not want to be called an author. He often said that a fellow who makes his living by writing should be called a writer, not an author. To him "author" suggested somebody recumbent on some lofty intellectual plateau. Somehow that idea always seemed a bit strange to me, coming from a fellow with one of the sharpest intellects I have ever encountered.

You will perceive that I speak here today mostly about Michener the man rather than about Michener's accomplishments. The reason for that is simply that people who knew him saw him as a warm, generous, considerate person—not as the winner of the Pulitzer Prize or the recipient of the Presidential Medal of Freedom. . . .

In the first place, he was a member of a team. And the other part of that team was his well-loved wife, Mari . . . She was a strong figure in Michener's life, and to see them together was to know that a good marriage could be a good friendship. She helped in building the art collection, she protected him when he needed protecting, and she goaded him when he needed goading, just as he curbed her when she needed curbing. Each gave first place to the other, and they called each other "Cookie."

The second thing I want to say about Michener has to do with religion. I went to him one day, not long ago, and said to him, "Jim, you grew up a Quaker, but in several of your books you celebrate the use of force. In these recent years you have become attached to this Presbyterian Church, but you have never conducted yourself as though your fate was predestined. So, my question to you is—do you consider yourself a religious man?" "Well," he said, "I've never been very faithful or sanctimonious, but I place a high value on the Bible and I have tried to conduct myself in ways that it prescribes. If you'd like to see the passage that has guided my life, look in the Second Book of James." So I did, and what I found there was the clear-cut insistence that faith alone is not enough, and that man must be judged by his deeds. And I put it to you now that nothing could characterize Michener's behavior better than the prescription that a man is to be judged by deeds as well as faith. For Michener's deeds have enriched the world and thousands of people in it.

Third, I must stress his belief in education, which was a major purpose in his life. He pursued that purpose in many places and in many ways. He taught in schools and universities, and he shared with them what he always considered his lucky and astonishing financial success. But he pursued that educational purpose in his books as well, for in them he was as much the teacher as he was the teller of tales—to which I must add that as a teller of tales the world has seldom seen the like of him.

And in the telling of his tales, he manifested a fourth quality that I must mention, and that is his feeling for the oppressed and the depressed. In many of his novels—in *Hawaii*, in *Texas*, in *The Convenant*, in *Sayonara*, in *The Bridge at Andau*, and others—his sympathy for the underdog is made clear, and his outrage at the injustice imposed upon one people by another becomes a kind of hallmark of his literary effort. As a writer and as a human being, Jim Michener was a liberal in the finest sense of that fine old term. He believed in liberty, in law, and in human rights, and in many of his tales he made that concern a central theme. . . .

So there have been many Micheners, and today we celebrate them all. The consummate professional, the broad-ranging intellect, the writer, the philanthropist, the complete human being, the friend of man. In many ways he will always be with us, but the truth is that he's gone and there is no way and no reason to avoid saying, "We'll miss you, Jim Michener." Looking at this beautiful lei on his likeness, I am moved to say "Aloha, Jim." We thank you, and we wish you well.

MALCOLM X
by Ossie Davis

Malcolm X (1925–1965) was born in Omaha, Nebraska, to Rev. Earl and Louise Little, members of Marcus Garvey's Universal Negro Improvement Association, a group that advocated black independence from whites. After a series of menial jobs, Malcolm drifted about New York and Boston as a drug dealer and burglar, eventually ending up in jail, where he discovered the Lost-Found Nation of Islam, a Muslim religious organization whose members believe in racial separation as the means to black freedom. Upon his release he became a minister for the group. But in 1963, after reevaluating its extremist nature, Malcolm broke from the Nation of Islam and the following year formed his own activist society, the Organization of Afro-American Unity. Several months later, in 1965, he was assassinated. Three black Muslim men were eventually convicted and sentenced for his murder.

Author, actor, and activist Ossie Davis was a very close friend of Malcolm X and gave the eulogy at his funeral, which took place at the Faith Temple Church of God on February 27. More than three decades later, in June 1997, Davis spoke at the funeral of Betty Shabazz, the widow of Malcolm X, saying, "Go well, sister Betty. Your journey ends and Malcolm steps from the shadows to greet his much beloved fresh from yesterday's deep and pain-filled river. Malcolm will embrace you and kiss you and whisper in your ear, 'Well done, Betty.' "

Here—at this final hour, in this quiet place—Harlem has come to bid farewell to one of its brightest hopes extinguished now, and gone from us forever. For Harlem is where he worked and where he struggled and fought—his home of homes, where his heart was, and where his people are—and it is, therefore, most fitting that we meet once again—in Harlem—to share these last moments with him. For Harlem has ever been gracious to those who have loved her, have fought for her, and have defended her honor even to the death. It is not in the

memory of man that this beleaguered, unfortunate, but nonetheless proud community has found a braver, more gallant
young champion than this Afro-American who lies before us—
unconquered still. I say the word again, as he would want me to:
Afro-American—Afro-American Malcolm, who was a master,
was most meticulous in his use of words. Nobody knew better
than he the power words have over the minds of men.

Malcolm had stopped being a "Negro" years ago. It had
become too small, too puny, too weak a word for him. Malcolm
was bigger than that. Malcolm had become an Afro-American
and he wanted—so desperately—that we, that all his people,
would become Afro-Americans too. There are those who will
consider it their duty, as friends of the Negro people, to tell us to
revile him, to flee, even from the presence of his memory, to
save ourselves by writing him out of the history of our turbulent
times.

Many will ask what Harlem finds to honor in this stormy, con-
troversial, and bold young captain—and we will smile. Many
will say turn away—away from this man, for he is not a man but
a demon, a monster, a subverter and an enemy of the black
man—and we will smile. They will say that he is of hate—a
fanatic, a racist—who can only bring evil to the cause for which
you struggle! And we will answer and say to them: Did you ever
talk to Brother Malcolm? Did you ever touch him, or have him
smile at you? Did you ever really listen to him? Did he ever do a
mean thing? Was he ever himself associated with violence or
any public disturbance? For if you did you would know him.
And if you knew him you would know why we must honor him:
Malcolm was our manhood, our living, black manhood! This
was his meaning to his people. And, in honoring him, we honor
the best in ourselves.

Last year, from Africa, he wrote these words to a friend: "My
journey," he says,

> is almost ended, and I have a much broader scope than when I
> started out, which I believe will add new life and dimension to
> our struggle for freedom and honor and dignity in the States. I

am writing these things so that you will know for a fact the tremendous sympathy and support we have among the African States for our Human Rights struggle. The main thing is that we keep a United Front wherein our most valuable time and energy will not be wasted fighting each other.

However we may have differed with him—or with each other about him and his value as a man—let his going from us serve only to bring us together, now. Consigning these mortal remains to earth, the common mother of all, secure in the knowledge that what we place in the ground is no more now a man—but a seed, which, after the winter of our discontent, will come forth again to meet us. And we will know him then for what he was and is—a Prince—our own black shining Prince!— who didn't hesitate to die, because he loved us so.

YITZHAK RABIN
by King Hussein

*Israeli Prime Minister and Defense Minister Yitzhak Rabin (1922–
1995) was shot to death in November 1995. His assassination at the
hand of a Jewish ultra-nationalist came in the wake of enormous
friction between the extremists and the more moderate segments of the
Jewish Israeli populations, who see the need for compromise and con-
cessions to achieve a peaceful co-existence with the Palestinians. The
assassination of Rabin, who fought tirelessly for Israeli-Arab rap-
prochement, derailed the peace process, setting back the chance to end the
violence in the Middle East.*

*There were endless mourners, some for the loss of the man, others for
the closing of his personal mission of reconciliation. Two eulogies from
his funeral, which took place on Mount Herzl in Jerusalem on November 6, 1995, are included here. His Majesty King Hussein of Jordan
delivered a powerful tribute to his former enemy, a man who had
become his trusted friend. Several months later Hussein said, "From
my point of view a great man fell on the other side, and his fall was a
great loss to the peace process and we are still suffering from the effect."
The second selection is from Rabin's granddaughter Noa Ben Artzi-
Pelossof. When she spoke these emotional words, her listeners could
hardly help but weep with her. This eulogy is unique in that it is in honor
of a military great spoken from the sweetness and sadness of a granddaughter's broken heart.*

My sister, Mrs. Leah Rabin, my friends, I had never
thought that the moment would come like this when I would
grieve the loss of a brother, a colleague, and a friend—a man, a
soldier who met us on the opposite side of a divide whom we
respected as he respected us. A man I came to know because I
realized, as he did, that we have to cross over the divide, estab-
lish a dialogue, get to know each other and strive to leave, for

those who follow us, a legacy that is worthy of them. And so we did. And so we became brethren and friends.

I've never been used to standing, except with you next to me, speaking of peace, speaking about dreams and hopes for generations to come that must live in peace, enjoy human dignity, come together, work together, to build a better future, which is their right. Never in all my thoughts would it have occurred to me that my first visit to Jerusalem in response to your invitation, the invitation of the Speaker of the Knesset, the invitation of the president of Israel, would be on such an occasion.

You lived as a soldier, you died as a soldier for peace . . . We belong to the camp of peace. We believe in peace. We believe that our one God wishes us to live in peace and wishes peace upon us, for these are His teachings to all the followers of the three great monotheistic religions, the children of Abraham. Let us not keep silent. Let our voices rise high to speak of our commitment to peace for all time to come, and let us tell those who live in darkness who are the enemies of life that through faith and religion and the teachings of our one God, this is where we stand . . . we are not ashamed, nor are we afraid, nor are we anything but determined to fulfill the legacy for which my friend fell, as did my grandfather in this very city when I was with him and but a young boy.

He was a man of courage, a man of vision and he was endowed with one of the greatest virtues that any man can have. He was endowed with humility. He felt with those around him and, in a position of responsibility, he placed himself, as I do and have done, often, in the place of the other partner to achieve a worthy goal. And we achieved peace, an honorable peace and a lasting peace. He had courage, he had vision, and he had a commitment to peace, and standing here, I commit before you, before my people in Jordan, before the world, myself to continue with our utmost, to ensure that we leave a similar legacy. And when my time comes, I hope it will be like my grandfather's and like Yitzhak Rabin's.

May your spirit rise high and may it sense how the people of

Jordan, my family, the people of Israel, decent people throughout the world feel today. So many live and so many inevitably
die. This is the will of God. This is the way of all, but those who
are fortunate and lucky in life are those who are greater, those
who leave something behind, and you are such a man, my
friend. The faces in my country amongst the majority of my
people and our armed forces and people who once were your
enemies are somber today and their hearts are heavy. Let us
hope and pray that God will give us all guidance, each in his
respective position to do what he can for the better future that
Yitzhak Rabin sought with determination and courage. As long
as I live, I'll be proud to have known him, to have worked with
him, as a brother and as a friend, and as a man, and the relationship of friendship that we had is something unique and I am
proud of that.

On behalf of the people of Jordan, my large Jordanian family,
my Hashemite family, to all those who belong to the camp of
peace, our deepest sympathies, our deepest condolences as we
share together this moment of remembrance and commitment,
to continue our struggle for the future of generations to come, as
did Yitzhak Rabin, and to fulfill his legacy.

YITZHAK RABIN
by Noa Ben Artzi-Pelossof

Please excuse me for not wanting to talk about the peace. I want to talk about my grandfather.

You always awake from a nightmare, but since yesterday I have been continually awakening to a nightmare. It is not possible to get used to the nightmare of life without you. The television never ceases to broadcast pictures of you, and you are so alive that I can almost touch you—but only almost, and I won't be able to anymore.

Grandfather, you were the pillar of fire in front of the camp and now we are left in the camp alone, in the dark; and we are so cold and so sad. I know that people talk in terms of a national tragedy, and of comforting an entire nation, but we feel the huge void that remains in your absence when grandmother doesn't stop crying. Few people really knew you. Now they will talk about you for quite some time, but I feel that they really don't know just how great the pain is, how great the tragedy is; something has been destroyed.

Grandfather, you were and still are our hero. I want you to know that every time I did anything, I saw you in front of me. Your appreciation and your love accompanied us every step down the road, and our lives were always shaped by your values. You, who never abandoned anything, are now abandoned. And here you are, my ever-present hero, cold, alone, and I cannot do anything to save you. You are missed so much.

Others greater than I have already eulogized you, but none of them ever had the pleasure I had to feel the caresses of your arms, your soft hands, to merit your warm embrace that was reserved only for us, to see your half-smile that always told me so much, that same smile which is no longer, frozen in the grave with you.

I have no feelings of revenge because my pain and feelings of loss are so large, too large. The ground has been swept out from below us, and we are groping now, trying to wander about in this empty void, without any success so far.

I am not able to finish this; left with no alternative, I say good-bye to you, hero, and ask you to rest in peace and think about us, and miss us, as down here we love you so very much. I imagine angels are accompanying you now, and I ask them to take care of you because you deserve their protection.

We will love you, Saba, forever.

A. BARTLETT GIAMATTI
by Marcus Giamatti

*A. Bartlett Giamatti (1938–1989) was one of America's leading schol-
ars in Renaissance English and comparative literature. He authored
books on Dante and Spenser and, in 1978, at the age of forty, became
the president of Yale University, the youngest in the school's two-
hundred-year history. Then, in 1986, Giamatti, who was a lifelong
sports fan, gave up his brilliant academic career to become the president
of baseball's National League, and was eventually appointed Commis-
sioner of Baseball. Sports fans best remember him for taking on baseball manager and former player Pete Rose, whom he banned from
baseball for life.*

*When Giamatti died, at the early age of fifty-one, a private graveside
service was held at the Grove Street Cemetery in New Haven, Connecti-
cut. At a public memorial service held for him at Yale's Woolsey Hall,
his eldest son, Marcus, remembered his father.*

In the third chapter of his last book, my father writes: "So
home drew Odysseus—who then set off again, because it is not
necessary to be in a specific place, in a house or town, to be one
who has gone home. So home is the goal—rarely glimpsed,
almost never attained—of all the heroes descended from Odysseus. All literary romance derives from the *Odyssey* and is about
rejoining. . . ."

My father—the idealist and the epical romantic—was not
unlike Odysseus; for A. Bartlett Giamatti, too, had "a driving
necessity" always to go out, along "routes full of turnings, wanderings, dangers," and always to come home again—because
that was where life "mattered most." At home, my father might
play, he might sleep, he might restore, and he might plan his
work—all the while rejoining with the family that he loved.

As his first-born son (Telemachus, if you will), I can remember home on Central Avenue in the Westville section of New

Haven. Yes, when I was age four, and five, and six, I would sit on my father's knee, in his favorite overstuffed, scarred leather chair. And he would read to me from a simple adaptation of Edmund Spenser's *Faerie Queene* about "St. George and the Dragon." And he would ramble mysteriously on about the Dream, the Flight, the Quest.

"Marcus" (his eyes would widen magically and he'd bare his awesome teeth), "this noble knight, riding swiftly on the plain, this Red Cross knight is on a great adventure bound, sent by Gloriana, to try his untried might." Then Dad might glower— and I would always be in awe—and he would whisper ominously: "A dreadful enemy awaits him—a Foul Friend—a dragon dangerous and frightful to behold." And thus he would begin again to teach me—to believe in myself, to be resourceful and resilient, and to carry on the fight. He would have so much fun with me when he read "St. George." He would act out all the parts, and he would allow me to dream, because he was dreaming, too.

At home again, at age ten and twelve and fourteen, I would play baseball with my father on the green patch of the pastorale which was our backyard. And just as he had done with the tall-tale telling of "St. George and the Dragon," A. Bartlett Giamatti would immerse himself in his role as instructor (or better still this time, coach), with the same passion, concentration, and desire to persuade. I can see him, forever in his uniform; that is, the faded red chino pants that were too short around the ankles, and the worn but polished buckle-shoes, and his Co-Op button-down, and his trusty Red Sox cap . . . His brow furrowed, he would scrutinize my "stance" at home plate . . . And with his usual unusual intensity, he would instruct: "Marcus! Concentrate your forces! Focus! Keep your eye on the ball! It's just like anything else." Or, "Marcus! When you take a cut at the ball, swing with all your might! Remember, every stroke is a new time—a second chance; learn from the mistakes you made the last time. One of these days, you'll hit the ball right out of the park! It's just like anything else." Or, "Marcus! Never argue with the umpire! Try to understand him; remember that he has an important job to do; he keeps and protects the laws of the game. It's just like anything else." . . .

And one final example of my father at home . . . in his cavernous study between the first and second floors: I, at age sixteen, seventeen, and onwards would marvel at my father at his desk and with his ever-present coffee mug rising occasionally to his determined lips as he labored lovingly, as he planned, strategized, and executed his next imagined journey . . . And as he guided the ballpoint pen—his trusty sword—easily navigating along the lines of the pages of his yellow legal pad, he'd often pause, lifting his head, his ears alert for inspiration; and he would assimilate the strains of music—Aretha Franklin or Willie Nelson—or maybe this time, Ray Charles—the singing of songs on the stereo—especially "Amazing Grace," which was his favorite. And as he created on paper, A. Bartlett Giamatti (I was always sure) was on another quest—with words; on one more journey that would (I always knew) bring at least some small measure of enlightenment into the darkening world. . . .

. . . My mother, my sister, my brother, and I loved him very much. . . .

Let no one say "There are no more heroes." My father is my hero. . . .

DR. MARTIN LUTHER KING, JR.
by Reverend Ralph D. Abernathy

Civil rights leader Dr. Martin Luther King, Jr. (1929–1968) was the voice of anguish and courage for a nation torn apart by segregation. When racial warfare was at its peak, he seemed to be the one man who could preserve the bridge of communication between the races, as he called for nonviolence and racial brotherhood.

King was shot to death on April 4, 1968, as he stood on the balcony of his motel room in Memphis, Tennessee, while there in support of the city's striking sanitation workers. He was aware of the threats against his life but said that it was not the future with which he was concerned as he had already seen the fulfillment of his goals. The night before he died, he said to a group of supporters, "It really doesn't matter what happens now . . . I've been to the mountaintop."

Millions of people mourned his death and tens of thousands attended his funeral, which was held in Atlanta, Georgia. His mahogany coffin made its way through the city on a crude farm wagon pulled by two mules, symbols of King's identification with the poor. The funeral service was held at the Ebenezer Baptist Church, after which a memorial service was held at Morehouse College. Reverend Ralph D. Abernathy, the fiery Baptist minister and leader of the struggle for civil rights, eulogized Dr. King.

. . . To be honored by being requested to give the eulogy at the funeral of Dr. Martin Luther King is like asking one to eulogize his deceased son, so close and so precious was he to me. Our friendship goes back to his student days here at Morehouse. It is not an easy task. Nevertheless I accepted with a sad heart and with full knowledge of my inadequacy to do justice to this good man.

It was my desire that if I predeceased Dr. King he would pay tribute to me on my final day. It was his wish that if he predeceased me I would deliver the homily at his funeral. Fate has decreed that I eulogize him. I wish it might have been otherwise for after all I am three score years and ten and Martin Luther is dead at thirty-nine.

How strange. God called the grandson of a slave on his father's side and the grandson of man born during the Civil War on his mother's side and said to him, "Martin Luther—Speak to America about war and peace. Speak to America about social justice and racial discrimination. Speak to America about nonviolence."

Let it be thoroughly understood that our deceased brother did not embrace nonviolence out of fear or cowardice. Moral courage was one of his noblest virtues. As Mahatma Gandhi challenged the British empire without a sword and won, Martin Luther challenged the interracial injustice of his country without a gun. He had faith to believe that he would win the battle for social justice.

I make bold to assert that it took more courage for Martin Luther to practice nonviolence than it took his assassin to fire the fatal shot. The assassin is a coward. He committed his dastardly deed and fled. When Martin Luther disobeyed an unjust law, he suffered the consequences of his action. He never ran away and he never begged for mercy. . . .

Coupled with moral courage was Martin Luther, Jr.'s, capacity to love people. Though deeply committed to a program of freedom for Negroes, he had a love and a deep concern for all kinds of people. He drew no distinction between the high and the low, none between the rich and the poor. He believed especially that he was sent to champion the cause of the man farthest down. He would probably have said, "If death had to come I am sure there was no greater cause to die for than fighting to get a just wage for garbage collectors."

This man was suprarace, supranation, supradenomination, supraclass, and supraculture. He belonged to the world and to mankind. Now he belongs to posterity.

But there is a dichotomy in all of this. This man was loved by some and hated by others. If any man knew the meaning of suffering, Martin Luther knew—house bombed; living day by day for thirteen years under constant threat of death; maliciously accused of being a Communist; falsely accused of being insecure, insincere, and seeking the limelight for his own glory; stabbed by a member of his own race; slugged in a hotel lobby; jailed thirty times; occasionally deeply hurt because his friends betrayed him.

And yet this man had no bitterness in his heart, no rancor in his soul, no revenge in his mind, and he went up and down the length and breadth of this world preaching nonviolence and the receptive power of love.

He believed with all of his heart, mind, and soul that the way to peace and brotherhood is through nonviolence, love, and suffering. He was severely criticized for his opposition to the war in Vietnam. It must be said, however, that one could hardly expect a prophet of King's commitment to advocate nonviolence at home and violence in Vietnam. Nonviolence to King was total commitment not only in solving the problems of race in the United States but in solving the problems of the world.

Surely, surely this man was called of God to his work. If Amos and Micah were prophets in the eighth century B.C., Martin Luther King, Jr., was a prophet in the twentieth century. If Isaiah was called of God to prophesy in his day, Martin Luther was called of God to prophesy in his day. If Hosea was sent to preach love and forgiveness centuries ago, Martin Luther was sent to expound the doctrine of nonviolence and forgiveness. . . . If Jesus was called to preach the Gospel to the poor, Martin Luther was called to bring dignity to the common man. . . .

What can we do? If we love Martin Luther King and respect him as this crowd surely testifies, let us see to it that he did not die in vain. Let us see to it that we do not dishonor his name by trying to solve our problems through rioting in the streets.

Violence was foreign to his nature. He warned that continued riots could produce a Fascist state. But let us see to it also that the conditions that cause riots are promptly removed as the president of the United States is trying to do. Let black and white alike search their hearts and if there be any prejudice in our hearts against interracial or ethnic groups let us exterminate it and let us pray as Martin Luther would pray if he could: "Father, forgive them, for they know not what they do." . . .

I close by saying to you what Martin Luther King, Jr., believed: "If physical death was the price he had to pay to rid America of prejudice and injustice nothing could be more redemptive." And to paraphrase words of the immortal John Fitzgerald Kennedy, permit me to say that Martin Luther King, Jr.'s, unfinished work on earth must truly be our own.

DR. MARTIN LUTHER KING, JR.
by David Dinkins

David Dinkins, who would become the mayor of New York City, delivered this speech several days after Dr. King was assassinated.

Martin Luther King is dead now, and we, the mourners and losers, are left with his dreams—with decisions to make. He is dead now, and there are no words we can say for him, for he said his own. He is dead now, and any eulogy must be for us, the living.

Martin Luther King is dead now, so for him there is no tomorrow on this earth. But for us there are tomorrows and tomorrows. He painted a picture of what our tomorrows could be in his dream of America. This past weekend painted a picture of how that dream could become a nightmare should we lose sight of his principles.

Martin Luther King is dead now, but he left a legacy. He planted in all of us, black and white, the seeds of love of justice, of decency, of honor, and we must not fail to have these seeds bear fruit.

Martin Luther King is dead now, and there is only time for action. The time for debate, the time for blame, the time for accusation is over. Ours is a clear call to action. We must not only dedicate ourselves to great principles, but we must apply those principles to our lives.

Martin Luther King is dead now, and he is because he dared believe in nonviolence in a world of violence. Because he dared believe in peace in a world of conflict. He is dead now because he challenged all of us to believe in his dream.

Martin Luther King is dead now, and we cannot allow the substance of his dream to turn into the ashes of defeat. If we are to build a tribute to what he stood for, we must, each of us, stand for the same things.

Martin Luther King is dead now, and I ask each of you, the living, to join him and me, to go from this room and keep the dream alive. We must now commit ourselves, we must now work, we must now define what kind of America we are going to have—for unless we make his dream a reality we will not have an America about which to decide.

Martin Luther King is dead now—but he lives.

DANIEL WEBSTER
by Amasa McCoy

Daniel Webster (1782–1852) was one of the most prolific and engaging orators, jurists, and statesmen in American history. Webster was born a sickly child and spent most of his boyhood reading and developing his lifelong interest in literature. After graduating from Dartmouth College, he became a leading lawyer, arguing numerous cases before the Supreme Court. His orations defined constitutional law, established public policy on tariffs, secession, and slavery, and generally shaped the nation's character. He dedicated his life to public service, becoming a respected congressman and senator and serving as secretary of state under presidents Harrison, Tyler, and Fillmore.

There were many different memorial services when Webster died and several well-known people eulogized him. But Amasa McCoy, a professor of logic and rhetoric at the National Law School, gave a most poignant tribute at the Presbyterian Church in Ballston Spa, New York, on November 8, 1852. The eulogy was so well received that the **New York Express** *published it and wrote in its review: "We publish today a beautiful oration. . . . The style of the orator in the delivery was faultless, and so riveted was the attention of the vast audience, that a pin might have been heard to fall in any part of the edifice during the pronouncing of the eulogy."*

The tolling bells of twice ten thousand steeples proclaim that we have met with no ordinary loss. Populous and opulent cities, thousands of miles from each other, celebrate these obsequies with all that can engage the imagination and impress the heart. Even in a retired village . . . the citizens of Ballston Spa, without distinction of party . . . have assembled, under these sable hangings, to join in the sublime lament which is now being sung by the nation. These expressions of public sorrow, however numerous and solemn, can be of no use, it is true, to the dead. But they may justly administer to the consolation of the living. To echo words once uttered by those lips, which because they are sealed in death, we are now convened: the tears which flow, and the honors that are paid, when the founders of the Republic die, give hope that the Republic itself will be immortal.

Daniel Webster, Secretary of State in the United States, died at his farm at Marshfield, on the morning of the 24th of October. Just ten days ago, his mortal remains were laid away in his family vault. . . . He was born, he lived, he died, in a century and a country of freedom. He first saw the light amid her mountain home, and he died where she lifts her radiant form to enjoy the ocean breeze. . . .

. . . Mr. Webster was not a man whose fame grew up overnight. He owed his eminence to no accident, no compromise of factions, no chance of battle, no freak of fortune. None of his influence was acquired by flattering the people, but only by serving them. . . . The explanation of Mr. Webster's fame consists simply in wonderful native endowments, disciplined by the last severity of culture and displayed in professional and public service. To eloquence, to law, to civil polity, he devoted more study than most public men to all united. If Buffon, as he said, owed ten or twelve volumes of his writings to his servant, who forced him to rise at six, it would be interesting—if it could be ascertained—to know what proportion of Mr. Webster's greatness is ascribable to his having risen at four.

The extinction of this great light afflicts no class more sorely than that scattered brotherhood who make up the republic of letters. In our part of that realm he was chief. No other man in this country ever exercised in so large a measure that sway over the human mind which belongs to literature. . . .

More than any other American of his day, more than any Englishman, Mr. Webster's style was chaste, lucid, and perspicuous. Every sentence was a crystal. He scattered among the people no ambiguous words. When Webster had spoken, you might differ from him indeed; but you knew his meaning. Whatever he touched, he not only adorned, but he shed over it a perpetual light. Such was the literary excellence of Mr. Webster's speech, that its influence did not cease with its delivery. There was always a charm over the printed report, that attracted and captivated innumerable readers . . . When it was known that Webster was to speak, is it any exaggeration to say that the Republic was one eager auditory? Give me a name if ye can, for glory like this: never to have risen, but millions hung upon his lips; never to have sat down, but millions were wiser men and better patriots. Webster's printed speeches were re-read, and put carefully away and committed. How many of his sentences, laden with noble truth and glowing patriotism, have become household words! Plutarch informs us that so thoroughly were the priests instructed in the writings of Numa, that the lawgiver, assured that they would be preserved in spirit and in letter, ordered them to be burned with his body. Such is the impression made upon the minds of his countrymen by the productions of Mr. Webster, that had all written record of them been interred with his remains, every principle and precept could be collected from the memory of living men; and all his great orations, I doubt not, could be restored to print, word for word. . . .

Cicero thought Socrates used such language as Jupiter would, had he talked in the Greek. The English of Webster suggests the same notion of majesty. And if Cicero had given us his idea of the fabled deity in the act and attitude of speaking, it is by no means certain that he would have invested him with a more imposing presence. . . .

. . . His published arguments at the bar have never yet been spoken of as less than consummate models of forensic discussion. And the proportion of his admirers is not small who insist that this is the theatre where the prowess of his mind achieved its greatest feats. As has been said by an old man eloquent, a patriarch of college presidents, respecting Hamilton: he strode through the cause with the club of Hercules, and left nothing living in his path. . . .

. . . Daniel Webster is no longer among the living. The glory of the forum, the chief of the Senate, the mighty minister, great man of language, "Farewell, a long farewell, to all thy greatness!" That drama of vigorous heroism is closed. On a stage, not darkened, but rather of heightened splendor, the curtain has fallen. Not as the ordinary great; nor yet as Socrates, like a philosopher; but with the sublimer exit of a Christian, he has gone from our sight forever. . . .

I know indeed the last accents of his lips— "I still live," and I have marked with sensibility the eagerness of the nation to extract from them something to solace its smitten feelings. Already in the valley of the shadow of death, it was in his mind only that the soul had not yet glided from the shore of its mortality. . . . The bleeding heart of the nation, so lonesome and desolate, is surely warranted in cherishing such a sentiment. All that was mortal of Daniel Webster is indeed dead. . . .

RAPHAEL SOYER
by Chaim Gross

Raphael Soyer (1899–1987) was a gifted painter who advocated realism at a time when abstract painting was the mode. He was known for his self-portraits and portraits of friends and female nudes. Some of his best-loved works are depression-era paintings of men out of work and New York's poor. He had his first one-man exhibition in 1929 and over the years won several awards for his work.

Chaim Gross, one of the most highly regarded sculptors of early twentieth-century American art, was Raphael Soyer's very close, lifelong friend. Their seventy-eight-year friendship began soon after Gross emigrated from East Austria, now Poland, to the United States, when the entire Soyer family embraced him as one of their own. It ended only with Soyer's death, upon which Gross paid this tribute to his muchmissed friend.

When you lose a friend like Raphael Soyer, you lose half of your body, half of your mind. We were friends, and we were very good friends since 1921 when I had arrived in America. I was seventeen years old and studying art when I met Moses Soyer at the Educational Alliance Art School. . . . Moses was the only one in my class who spoke Yiddish and my only language was Yiddish. We took many walks together, and he taught me English.

The Soyer family had come from Russia in 1912. Their first home in New York was in the Bronx. They were very poor. Moses brought me home to his house on Boone Avenue and I became friends with his twin brother, Raphael, his sisters, his brother Isaac, his mama and papa, and grandmother; I was just one of them. I could come up any time and have a meal.

When we had free time, on Saturdays or Sundays, Raphael, Moses, Isaac, and I would go to Coney Island, or Sea Gate, or the Manhattan piers, or we would go all over the Bronx, every street. We drew and painted. . . .

Raphael Soyer was the last of his generation who was a great modern American painter, the period that bridged European traditional painting with American painting. He was on his own; he always stuck with what he was interested in. He survived the generation breaking with traditional past, and he survived to enjoy the renewed recognition as a forerunner of the youngest generation of realist painters. . . .

He always had his sketchbook. We all had sketchbooks. For everything we saw, we would do a sketch of it. He did the same thing. Everywhere he went, to the museum or in the streets. While he traveled, he met many artists and sketched them. Eventually, the sketchbook with his autobiography was published. . . .

He would often say to me, "Why did Moses have to die before me?"

In the last ten or fifteen years, there was a great change in his paintings. The colors became stronger and better, clearer, very beautiful blues and grays and yellows. His paintings were always mellow and beautiful.

In the last few summers Raphael came to Provincetown but in the last year, 1987, he was not quite himself. In past years, he would paint all the time. He didn't feel like painting. He felt like sitting, reading, drawing a little bit. We saw each other almost every day. . . . He never complained about anything. When he left Provincetown he was in perfect health. A few days later, he took sick. He went to the hospital. When I visited him a few days later, he was an entirely different person. I went to visit him at the hospital almost every day. When he came back home, I visited him at his house.

He would take me for a walk, and show me his collection. He would show me a drawing, and say, "Remember this drawing by Friedlander?" or "Remember when you made this drawing . . ." he had the drawing on his wall for so many years. . . .

Anybody who came to his bed, he would take them by the hand, press their hand, and tell them good-bye. He knew what was going on. Someone called from California, "Tell her the truth," he said—just like his paintings, always truthful.

When you lose a friend, you lose half your body, half of your mind; and the other half, you don't know what happens: Raphael Soyer was really my best friend. When you have a very close friend, he knows your secrets, and you know his secrets. This is how friends get along. He was on his own, different from all the others, always himself, always unique. It was really wonderful to have been with him.

ROBERT KENNEDY
by Edward Kennedy

There is little need to stress the horror when, for the second time in five years, a young, vibrant Kennedy was brutally assassinated. For many, Robert Kennedy (1925–1968) represented the essential decency of people and the hope for peaceful and intelligent change during a tumultuous time in American history. Kennedy was at the Ambassador Hotel in Los Angeles, where he had just announced his victory in the California Democratic primary, when he was shot twice in the head. After he collapsed his wife, Ethel, knelt by his side. Pleading with onlookers to move back, she placed her rosary beads in her dying husband's hands. Kennedy left behind ten children and his wife, who was pregnant with their eleventh child.

A short, private funeral was held at St. Patrick's Cathedral in New York City on June 8, 1968. After the Mass, his body was taken by train to Washington, D.C., where he was buried near his slain brother, John F. Kennedy, on a hillside at Arlington National Cemetery. Edward Kennedy, the last surviving Kennedy son, gave the eulogy.

On behalf of Mrs. Robert Kennedy, her children, and the parents and sisters of Robert Kennedy, I want to express what we feel to those who mourn with us today in this Cathedral and around the world. We loved him as a brother and father and son. From his parents, and from his older brothers and sisters—Joe, Kathleen, and Jack—he received inspiration which he passed on to all of us. He gave us strength in time of trouble, wisdom in time of uncertainty, and sharing in time of happiness. He was always by our side.

Love is not an easy feeling to put into words. Nor is loyalty, or trust, or joy. But he was all of these. He loved life completely and lived it intensely.

A few years back, Robert Kennedy wrote some words about

his own father and they expressed the way we in his family feel about him. He said of what his father meant to him:

> What it really all adds up to is love . . . the kind of love that is affection and respect, order, encouragement, and support. Our awareness of this was an incalculable source of strength, and because real love is something unselfish and involves sacrifice and giving, we could not help but profit from it. Beneath it all, he has tried to engender a social conscience. There were wrongs which needed attention. There were people who were poor and who needed help. And we have a responsibility to them and to this country. . . . We, therefore, have a responsibility to others who are less well off.

This is what Robert Kennedy was given. What he leaves us is what he said, what he did, and what he stood for. A speech he made to the young people of South Africa on their Day of Affirmation in 1966 sums it up the best, and I would read it now:

> There is a discrimination in this world and slavery and slaughter and starvation. Governments repress their people; and millions are trapped in poverty while the nation grows rich; and wealth is lavished on armaments everywhere.
>
> There are differing evils, but they are common works of man. They reflect the imperfection of human justice, the inadequacy of human compassion, our lack of sensibility toward the sufferings of our fellows.
>
> But we can perhaps remember—even if only for a time— that those who live with us are our brothers; that they share with us the same short moment of life; that they seek—as we do— nothing but the chance to live out their lives in purpose and happiness, winning what satisfaction and fulfillment they can.
>
> Surely this bond of common faith, this bond of common goal, can begin to teach us something. Surely, we can learn, at least, to look at those around us as fellow men. And surely we can begin to work a little harder to bind up the wounds among us

and to become in our own hearts brothers and countrymen once again.

Our answer is to rely on youth—not a time of life but a state of mind, a temper of the will, a quality of imagination, a predominance of courage over timidity, of the appetite for adventure over the love of ease. The cruelties of obstacles of this swiftly changing planet will not yield to obsolete dogmas and outworn slogans. They cannot be moved by those who cling to a present that is already dying, who prefer the illusion of security to the excitement and danger that come with even the most peaceful progress. . . .

Some believe there is nothing one man or one woman can do against the enormous array of the world's ills. Yet many of the world's great movements, of thought and action, have flowed from the work of a single man. A young monk began the Protestant reformation, a young general extended an empire from Macedonia to the borders of the earth, and a young woman reclaimed the territory of France. It was a young Italian explorer who discovered the New World, and the thirty-two-year-old Thomas Jefferson who proclaimed that all men are created equal.

These men moved the world, and so can we all. Few will have the greatness to bend history itself, but each of us can work to change a small portion of events, and in the total of all those acts will be written the history of this generation. It is from numberless diverse acts of courage and belief that human history is shaped. Each time a man stands up for an ideal, or acts to improve the lot of others, or strikes out against injustice, he sends forth a tiny ripple of hope, and crossing each other from a million different centers of energy and daring, those ripples build a current that can sweep down the mightiest walls of oppression and resistance.

Few are willing to brave the disapproval of their fellows, the censure of their colleagues, the wrath of their society. Moral courage is a rarer commodity than bravery in battle or great intelligence. Yet it is the one essential, vital quality for those who seek to change a world that yields most painfully to change. . . .

Our future may lie beyond our vision, but it is not completely beyond our control. It is the shaping impulse of America that neither fate nor nature nor the irresistible tides of history, but the work of our own hands, matched to reason and principle, that will determine our destiny. There is pride in that, even arrogance, but there is also experience and truth. In any event, it is the only way we can live.

This is the way he lived. My brother need not be idealized, or enlarged in death beyond what he was in life, to be remembered simply as a good and decent man, who saw wrong and tried to right it, saw suffering and tried to heal it, saw war and tried to stop it.

Those of us who loved him and who take him to his rest today pray that what he was to us and what he wished for others will some day come to pass for all the world. As he said many times, in many parts of this nation, to those he touched and who sought to touch him:

Some men see things as they are and say why.
I dream things that never were and say why not?

JACQUELINE KENNEDY ONASSIS
by Maurice Tempelsman

It is fitting that a tribute is chosen here for a woman who truly knew the meaning of honoring the dead. Jacqueline Kennedy Onassis (1929–1994) displayed remarkable fortitude and presence of mind when her husband, President John Kennedy, was assassinated in November 1963. While it would have been entirely appropriate for her to select several family or staff members to arrange the president's funeral, Mrs. Kennedy insisted on orchestrating an elegant, emotional ceremony that she hoped would console an entire nation. Most of the funeral details were her ideas, many of which were taken from a close study of the funeral of Abraham Lincoln, which she undertook the day after her husband's murder. She chose to walk the eight blocks behind the cortege to the cathedral; she insisted that her husband be buried in Arlington National Cemetery rather than at the Kennedy family plot in Brookline, Massachusetts, and she ordered the lighting of an eternal flame in her husband's memory. Many remember the now iconic black mourning veil she chose to wear, which covered her entire head.

Through the assassination, her unexpected second marriage to Greek shipping mogul Aristotle Onassis, the raising of her children as a single mother, and her brave battle with cancer, Jacqueline Kennedy Onassis remained courageous and dignified. Although she was an object of fascination, she was an intensely private person and gave her last interview nearly thirty years before her death. Her private funeral was held at the Church of St. Ignatius Loyola in New York City on May 23, 1994. Her longtime companion Maurice Tempelsman chose to read "Ithaka" by C. P. Cavafy and ended his farewell with a few simple words.

Laistrygonians and Cyclops, angry Poseidon—don't be afraid of them: you'll never find things like that on your way as long as you keep your thoughts raised high, as long as a rare excitement stirs your spirit and your body.
Laistrygonians and Cyclops, wild Poseidon—you won't en-

counter them unless you bring them along inside your soul, unless your soul sets them up in front of you.

Hope the voyage is a long one.

May there be many a summer morning when, with what pleasure, what joy, you come into harbors seen for the first time; may you stop at Phoenician trading stations to buy fine things, mother of pearl and coral, amber and ebony, sensual perfume of every kind—as many sensual perfumes as you can, and may you visit many Egyptian cities to gather stores of knowledge from their scholars.

Keep Ithaka always in your mind. Arriving there is what you are destined for.

But do not hurry the journey at all.

Better if it lasts for years, so you are old by the time you reach the island, wealthy with all you have gained on the way, not expecting Ithaka to make you rich.

Ithaka gave you the marvelous journey. Without her, you would not have set out.

She has nothing left to give you now.

And if you find her poor, Ithaka won't have fooled you.

Wise as you will have become, so full of experience, you will have understood by then what these Ithakas mean.

Tempelsman concluded in his own words:

And now the journey is over, too short, alas, too short. It was filled with adventure and wisdom, laughter and love, gallantry and grace. So farewell, farewell.

CLARA M. HALE
by Reverend James A. Forbes, Jr.

Clara M. Hale (1906–1992) originally decided to become a foster parent after her husband, Thomas, died, leaving her to care for her three young children alone. Over the years she fostered more than forty youngsters. In 1969, "Mother," as she was affectionately and respectfully called by everyone who knew her, set up Hale House, a haven for drug- and AIDS-infected babies whose parents were temporarily unable to care for them. Her homespun prescription for nurturing children was "to hold them, rock them, love them, and tell them how great they are." At the time of her death, Mother Hale was an internationally known figure, praised around the world for her dedication to the young and needy. She left a legacy of love and devotion to countless children and their families. When she died the charismatic Reverend James A. Forbes, Jr., senior minister at the Riverside Church in Harlem, gave her this farewell.

Once upon a time, there lived a woman in Harlem, U.S.A., whose love for children was so strong that she could not bear to see them neglected, abandoned, mistreated, and abused. When crying and longing eyes reached out to her for help, her arms could not be restrained. She extended her heart and her love, her smiles and kisses and especially showed all her tender hands whose touch was like the balm of Gilead, an ointment of grace—like a massage with a comforting message. "You are so lovely: Why hasn't the whole world noticed?"

In her eyes children could see God's love announcing their specialness, and around the walls of her home, mirrors were placed just right so that no child would miss the beauty contest in which each entry was a winner.

She gave so much, but found such joy that others begged for a share in her hospitality for God's little ones. From all around the world they came or sent their tokens of care to Hale House.

Why? Because Mother Clara Hale had taught the world the power of tender loving care to turn obstacles into stepping stones to a healthy and productive life.

What an angel in our midst! She taught us the art of guiding little feet across bridges over troubled waters and landing them safe on a solid rock. She delivered everything God sent by her to us and then she returned to the God who had sent her with gifts so rich and rare.

Today, we come to celebrate the life, legacy, and faith which undergirded her unique ministry. We come to etch into our hearts and minds the godlike qualities we saw in her living color. We come to unveil a more lasting memorial, which will keep the story alive for generations to come.

So let us remember her instructions once again—"No sad and mournful gathering for me." There are too many victories to celebrate, too many joys to be shared along the way. So let there be music and children's voices and worlds of thanks and expressions of hope. Celebration is the order of the day. Let us pray.

Dear Lord, we thank you for Mother Clara Hale. Let this service of remembrance be true to the spirit of her life. May the work she has left behind find new strength, guidance, and willing hands to build upon a great tradition. Speak to the hearts of children so they will always remember how special they are and how they can make a difference in the world.

TERENCE MacSWINEY
by Eamon De Valera

Irish author Terence MacSwiney (1879–1920) was a playwright and a politician, but he was best known as a martyred revolutionary who fought for Ireland's right to independence. MacSwiney, who was Lord Mayor of Cork, was arrested, sentenced by a British court-martial, and imprisoned at Brixton Jail in London. In a dramatic demonstration of protest against British rule in Ireland, he refused food from the day of his arrest, and on the seventy-fourth day of his hunger strike, he starved to death.

MacSwiney's sacrifice focused world attention on the Irish struggle. His funeral was a day of national mourning and there were massive demonstrations in London and Cork. Eamon De Valera, an American-born Irish political leader, who went on to become the first president of the Republic of Ireland, gave this moving tribute to him. At the time of MacSwiney's death, De Valera was president of Sinn Fein.

England has killed another son for Ireland to mourn. She has robbed another woman of the joy of her life, and made another orphan sad for the father she must never know. And Lloyd George is proud of his work. Proud that he has given proof that the British empire is not done for yet—a proof that we do not gainsay, for it is truly a proof that convinces. In every generation for seven centuries Ireland's cry has necessarily been: it is a hard service they take that helps me. Many a child will be born, and there will be no father at the christening to give it a name. Many that have red cheeks now will have pale cheeks for my sake. And our children have never once feigned to respond. They offer themselves gladly for the sacrifice. MacSwiney and his comrades gave up their lives for their country. The English have killed them.

Tomorrow a boy, head and body, they will hang, and Hale-like, he will only regret that he has but one life to give. Oh God.

For they shall be alive forever; they shall be speaking forever; they shall be remembered forever; the people will hear them forever. Ye mothers that are here, think that each one of these too had a mother who loved him as you love your sons. Ye wives that are here, think that MacSwiney too had a wife, and her love was no less than yours. Ye children that are here, think that he too had a child, and his love was as kind as your fathers'. And they are dead that men should be at peace, and war should be no more, and that a small nation that covets nothing from its neighbor should enjoy the right of its own freedom.

But Ireland dries her tears over the graves of her martyred ones. They have fought their fight and they shall reap the victory. Lloyd George has killed them, but their bodies only had he reached, their spirits he could not. He has buried them by the peck; they have not been found wanting. Fitzgerald's and Mac-Swiney's and Murphy's bodies are indeed in the clay, but it is the sacred bosom of the motherland they loved so well and served so nobly, and their godlike spirits are with us now to inspire, and to be at our side always with a legioned strength to help us. If God wills that the freedom of our country should thus come in our own rather than in the blood of our enemies, we too shall not hesitate at the price, nor shrink at the sacrifice. Nor will those who come after us value less the heritage we shall thus have purchased for them. The glorious standards our comrades have set must be ours and in this last phase of Ireland's struggle, to which it has been their privilege to lead the van, our motto must be theirs—the motto of victory, liberty, or death.

GEORGE BURNS
by Irving Fein

Comedian George Burns (1896–1996) began his career on the vaude-ville stage. He was a pioneer in radio and TV and with his wife, Gracie Allen, he became a legend of the entertainment industry. At the age of eighty he received an Academy Award for his performance in the 1975 film **The Sunshine Boys**. *His recipe for long life was simple: "I like my food hot, I exercise, I smoke fifteen to twenty cigars a day and I dance very close." When he died at the age of one hundred, Burns' body was buried beside his beloved Gracie, whose loss he publicly mourned for over thirty-two years. Some sixty friends and family members attended the funeral, which was held at Forest Lawn Memorial Park in Glendale, California. His producer, Irving Fein, delivered the only eulogy. Fein said, "George didn't want a lot of people. He wanted it simple. So we kept it simple."*

Today we are here to pay our respects to one of the most beloved performers of the show business world. Everyone here knew him so long that there is very little I can say about this remarkable man that you don't already know. Singer . . . dancer . . . straight man . . . actor . . . comedian . . . author. He will leave a very large void in our lives. I knew George for fifty years and had the privilege of representing him for the last twenty-two, until he fell in 1994. What marvelous years they were.

One of the many things I admired about George was his absolute determination to keep doing what he loved best in the world: working in show business. Always on time (or early), always prepared, he never missed a single performance and was the consummate professional. And as the years advanced, and I would discuss his possible retirement, he would say "Retire? What am I supposed to do, stay home and play with my cuticles?" Or he'd say, "Quit? I can't quit. Who would support my mother and father?" It was that attitude, plus his many gifts, plus the love from his adoring fans coming across the footlights wherever he worked that enabled him to stay on top all those years.

George always gave Gracie credit for their success on stage. But he was the one who knew what would or wouldn't work. As he often said, he knew entrances and exits. And last Saturday, he knew it was time to go. He was here for one hundred great years. We may have wished for more but no one in this room could have wanted him to just hang on. Unable to hear the laughter and applause, or take his bows.

So, George, we'll miss you. I know you took your music with you. So wherever you are, I hope they're playing it in your key.

LAURENCE OLIVIER
by Bernard Levin

Many believe that Laurence Olivier (1907–1989), known for his spell-binding performances on stage and in film, was the most outstanding actor of his generation. From **Henry V** *to* **Wuthering Heights**, *his presence and talent held audiences in awe. Theater-goers who saw him deliver an opening soliloquy would often comment on his magnetism. Lord Olivier died peacefully in his sleep at the age of eighty-two. On the night of his death the Shakespeare Memorial Theatre and the National Theatre in London, of which he was the first director, flew their flags at half mast, and London's West End theaters switched off their outside lights. When his ashes were brought to rest at Westminster Abbey, his wife, actress Joan Plowright, chose this tribute, by writer Bernard Levin, to be read by actor Alan Bates, a family friend.*

Let us be clear about exactly what it is that we have lost with the death of Laurence Olivier. Theatre goers have lost the greatest of modern actors, and one of such gifts that perhaps only three or four in all history could have counted themselves his peers; but there is another category, and it is there that is the most impoverished by his passing, for he takes with him a quality that is now more rare, yet never more needed—than at any time in our history. What we have lost with Laurence Olivier is glory.

He reflected it in his greatest roles; indeed, he walked clad in it—you could practically see it glowing around him like a nimbus. He had a quality that he shared with some of the greatest men and women in this country's history, among whom he would have been welcome and at home: monarchs like Henry V and Elizabeth I, men of action like Marlborough and Drake, statesmen like Cecil and Disraeli, adventurer-artists like Ralegh and Sidney, creators like Van Dyck, Dickens, and Elgar, interpreters like Beecham, shapers of the cosmos like Newton and Hume, poets like Byron and Graves, historians like Clarendon and Macaulay, journalists like Hazlitt and Cobbett, orators like Fox and Churchill.

There is no name on that list that Olivier was unworthy to stand beside, and he and they have that quality of glory in common. With that list to provide a framework, it is possible to attempt a definition of it. Part of it is optimism—not the facile optimism that ignores reality but the profound kind that accepts it but believes that the world may yet be saved. "Clenching his fist at the deathpale stars," such an optimist faces always outwards, and in his heart it is always noon. . . . Such a picture points inevitably to further qualities. Chief among these is courage, and Olivier radiated it. . . . Optimism; courage; the third quality of glory is romanticism. Again, not the sentimental or bombastic kind, but the romanticism of those who live always above the clouds . . .

It adds up to glory: Laurence Olivier's work was glorious in the same ways as the Fifth Symphony of Beethoven is glorious, and we can say of it what E. M. Forster said of that music, that "all sorts and conditions are satisfied by it . . . the passion of your life becomes more vivid."

What a titanic figure he was! What a marvelous man! . . . No one will ever fill the place he leaves in the hearts of those who knew him; no one will ever play the roles he played as he played them; no one will replace the splendour that he gave his native land with his genius. . . .

This king among men is no more, and there is none to ascend the vacant throne. Roland's horn is silent; the lance of El Cid is couched; Don John of Austria rides home from the Crusade. Laurence Olivier—actor of genius, citizen of the world, hero of our time—home is gone, and ta'en his wages; golden boys and girls all must, like chimney-sweepers, come to dust. Let us ring down the curtain, switch off the lights, and tiptoe from the empty theatre.

The crown o' the earth doth melt. My Lord!
O! wither'd is the garland of the war,
The soldier's pole is fall'n: young boys and girls
Are level now with men; the odds is gone,
And there is nothing left remarkable
Beneath the visiting moon.

THOMAS JEFFERSON AND JOHN ADAMS
by Edward Everett

July 4, 1826, marked the fiftieth anniversary of the adoption of the Dec-
laration of Independence and in a nearly unbelievable coincidence both
Thomas Jefferson (1743–1826), aged eighty-three, and John Adams
(1735–1826), aged ninety-one, died that very day. Adams had been
asked to attend the anniversary festivities in his hometown of Quincy,
Massachusetts, but, weak and bedridden, he was unable to participate.
Seated by a window so that he could watch the activity on the streets
below, he was heard to say, "Jefferson still survives," and soon after
slipped into a state of unconsciousness. Little did Adams know that Jef-
ferson in fact had died earlier that day.

Years before, Jefferson had asked Adams if he feared death. Adams
responded that death "is not an evil. It is a blessing to the individual,
and to the world. Yet we ought not to wish for it till life becomes insup-
portable; we must wait the pleasure and convenience of this great
teacher." Jefferson agreed and in a letter wrote to Adams, "There is a
ripeness of time for death, regarding others as well as ourselves, when it
is reasonable we should drop off, and make room for another growth.
When we have lived our generation out, we should not wish to encroach
on another."

Edward Everett was a dazzling orator, respected for his brilliant
speech at the dedication of the Gettysburg Battlefield Cemetery in 1863.
But as a relatively young man, Everett delivered this memorable trib-
ute in honor of Adams and Jefferson several weeks after their deaths.
Everett went on to serve as governor of Massachusetts, ambassador to
Great Britain, and president of Harvard University.

. . . Fellow citizens, the great heads of the American family
are fast passing away; of the last, of the most honored, two are
now no more. We are assembled, not to gaze with awe on the
artificial and theatric images of their features, but to contem-
plate their venerated characters, to call to mind their invaluable

services, and to lay up the image of their virtues in our hearts. The two men who stood in a relation in which no others now stand to the whole Union, have fallen. . . .

They were useful, honored, prosperous and lovely in their lives, and in their deaths they were not divided. Happiest at the last, they were permitted almost to choose the hour of their departure; to die on that day on which those who loved them best could have wished they might die. . . .

The jubilee of America is turned into mourning. Its joy is mingled with sadness; its silver trumpet breathes a mingled strain. Henceforward, while America exists among the nations of the earth, the first emotion of the fourth of July will be of joy and triumph in the great event which immortalizes the day; the second will be one of chastened and tender recollection of the venerable men who departed on the morning of the jubilee. This mingled emotion of triumph and sadness has sealed the beauty and sublimity of our great anniversary. . . . Had our venerated fathers left us on any other day, it would have been henceforward a day of mournful recollection. But now, the whole nation feels, as with one heart, that since it must sooner or later have been bereaved of its revered fathers, it could not have wished that any other had been the day of their decease. Our anniversary festival was before triumphant; it is now triumphant and sacred. It before called out the young and ardent to join in the public rejoicing; it now also speaks, in a touching voice, to the retired, to the gray-headed, to the mild and peaceful spirits, to the whole family of sober freemen. It is full of greatness, and full of goodness. It is absolute and complete. The death of the men who declared our independence—their death on the day of the jubilee—was all that was wanting to the fourth of July. To die on that day, and to die together, was all that was wanting to Jefferson and Adams. . . .

Friends, fellow citizens, free, prosperous, happy Americans! The men who did so much to make you so are no more. The men who gave nothing to pleasure in youth, nothing to repose in age, but all to that country whose beloved name filled their hearts, as it does ours, with joy, can now do no more for us; nor we for them. But their memory remains, we will cherish it; their bright example remains, we will strive to imitate it; the fruit of their wise counsels and noble acts remains, we will gratefully enjoy it.

They have gone to the companions of their cares, of their dangers, and their toils. It is well with them. The treasures of America are now in heaven. How long the list of our good, and wise, and brave assembled there! How few remain with us! There is our Washington; and those who followed him in their country's confidence are now met together with him, and all their illustrious company.

The faithful marble may preserve their image; the engraven brass may proclaim their worth; but the humblest sod of Independent America, with nothing but the dewdrops of the morning to gild it, is a prouder mausoleum than kings or conquerors can boast. The country is their monument. Its independence is their epitaph. But not to their country is their praise limited. The whole earth is the monument of illustrious men. Wherever an agonizing people shall perish, in a generous convulsion, for want of a valiant arm and a fearless heart, they will cry, in the last accents of despair, O for a Washington, an Adams, a Jefferson! Wherever a regenerated nation, starting up in its might, shall burst the links of steel that enchain it, the praise of our venerated fathers shall be remembered in their triumphal song!

The contemporary and successive generations of men will disappear, and in the long lapse of ages, the races of America, like those of Greece and Rome, may pass away. The fabric of American freedom, like all things human, however firm and fair, may crumble into dust. But the cause in which these our fathers shone is immortal. They did that to which no age, no people of civilized men, can be indifferent. Their eulogy will be uttered in other languages, when those we speak, like us who speak them, shall be all forgotten. And when the great account of humanity shall be closed, in the bright list of those who have best adorned and served it shall be found the names of our Adams and our Jefferson!

ROBERT GWATHMEY
by Charles Gwathmey

Robert Gwathmey (1903–1988) was one of America's leading social realist painters. His major theme was the rural South of his childhood, and his depiction of sharecroppers and migrant workers revealed the South as a land of bigotry, exploitation, and hypocritical politicians. Although his style was characterized as cool, intellectual, and geometric, his paintings reveal his enormous concern for society's underprivileged. Throughout his adult life he was active in campaigns for artists' rights and larger social issues. Gwathmey also had a distinguished career at New York's Cooper Union for the Advancement of Science and Art, where he taught drawing for twenty-six years. When he died of Parkinson's disease at the age of eighty-five, a memorial service was held on April 5, 1989, at the Guild Hall in East Hampton, New York. His son, architect Charles Gwathmey, gave this poignant eulogy.

I dreaded the day of my father's death since I was old enough to comprehend the idea. Therefore, I wish to use this opportunity, somewhat selfishly, to frame a personal picture of Bob that will at least allow me to adjust to the deep sadness I feel and the loss I must reconcile.

Robert Gwathmey's father died before he was born, and he was raised by his mother and three older sisters, which had a major impact on the nature and quality of his fatherhood. I was, as the only child and son, the direct beneficiary of a most extraordinary upbringing that was both an example and a lesson in compassion, commitment, and devotion to art, ideals, fellow man, and family.

Bob was simply, from as far back as I can remember, my best friend. He was my father, but our life experience manifested itself in us sharing a private and exhilarating exploration that bound us, and still holds us in a unique and uncompromising place.

He believed that art must affect morality and conscience. It was a means of communicating both an idea and a hope. Life as an artist was contributive, noncompetitive, and uncompromising.

Bob painted at home. His studio was my classroom. I watched, talked, emulated, and envied. He was a craftsman and perfectionist who did not believe in the "sketch" per se, but in the "resolution." His self-criticism and intolerance for the "almost" was contagious and infectious. . . .

He saved time for me and was as insistent on its realization as he was about his work ethic. Every Monday night my mother, Rosalie, and I would meet Bob promptly at 6 o'clock at the Sea-Fair Restaurant on 8th Street, so we could be together before he taught school at Cooper Union, after having taught all day. He believed that anyone who could work at a job by day and still have the energy to attend night school to pursue art deserved his extended time and energy. . . .

Every Tuesday and Thursday night we walked from our apartment on 68th Street and Central Park West to the Translux Theatre on 52nd Street and Broadway to see the newsreel. We talked, looked in the appliance and car showroom windows, speculated and dreamt together. After the one-hour newsreel, we went to a bar on Eighth Avenue, where the bartender couldn't wait to see the man who told great jokes, wore tweed jackets and plaid shirts, and watched his little kid eat raw clams on the half shell.

On Wednesdays he had Artist Equity meetings at the apartment, where I could listen to his fellow artists and friends discuss the sociopolitical climate and problems of the times. I realized, even then, that I was a child sharing a different vision from the mainstream, where art and social consciousness were morally and intellectually integrated into our daily life and that one's self-esteem was worth suffering any consequences.

On Friday or Saturday night there was always a dinner

party or private fund-raiser for a fellow artist, writer, or actor to help defend him/her against the House Un-American Activities Committee or any other supportable left-wing or social-conscience cause. I ate early, but listened late, again realizing social-conscience values and commitments that were not simply accommodative but were life-determining.

Saturdays were for outings: college football games or track meets or basketball or baseball games and excursions to experience events, crowds, weather, travel, competition, and variety.

Sunday mornings . . . we took the subway to La Guardia Airport and watched the planes take off and land, again fulfilling our mutual fantasies and aspirations. Sunday afternoons were reserved for museums, I being the recipient of a continuous explanation of the history of art and cultures with descriptions of intentions and perceptions of paintings and sculptures through the eyes of my artist/teacher father.

He took me to see the movie *The Informer* when I was ten and to *The Grapes of Wrath* twice before I was twelve. We walked in the May Day parade every year, and I was always holding his hand as a participant in a picket line or a demonstration to protest a form of intellectual, social, or moral injustice.

I mention these reflections to illustrate a conclusion. I lived my early childhood with a father/friend who could not wait for me to be an adult (he shaved me when I was eleven) so that in some way he could see if he "did right" as a father, and then somehow reverse roles and relive a childhood he never experienced, through his son.

I feel privileged and humbled by my father's life example. It is continually inspirational and demanding. I love a man who always left more than he took, who believed passionately in the nobility of his fellow man, and who dignified compassion. I miss the one person who without question was my best friend in life and who remains my conscience in death.

STEPHEN BANTU BIKO
by Archbishop Desmond Tutu

In 1969 a group of students in South Africa formed the South African Students' Organization (SASO) to advocate black consciousness and defiance against apartheid. Stephen Bantu Biko (1946–1977), then a medical student, was chosen as the group's first president. Many of the SASO leaders were frequently harassed, detained, or arrested, and Stephen was picked up by the Security Police in Port Elizabeth on August 18, 1977. He was denied exercise and kept naked in a cell for eighteen days. On September 7 he suffered a brain injury from three blows to the head. For some unknown reason he was transported, while lying naked on the floor of a van, 750 miles to Pretoria. He died on September 12, leaving a wife and two sons, the tenth political prisoner to die in police custody that year alone.

Stephen Biko's outrageous fate focused worldwide attention on South Africa's legalized bigotry. Over 15,000 people came to pay their last respects on September 25 in King William's Town on the Eastern Cape. Several prominent activists and friends were actually banned from attending his funeral, which was as much a protest rally against white minority rule as a farewell to the young leader. In a unique show of support thirteen Western nations sent diplomats to the funeral. The top of Biko's coffin bore the symbol of black consciousness, two hands breaking the iron shackles binding them. The eulogy was delivered by Archbishop Desmond Tutu, the 1994 Nobel Peace Prize laureate, who was bishop of Lestho at the time of Biko's death. An outstanding leader in the struggle against apartheid, Tutu spoke passionately about Biko and forcefully about the need for change.

When we heard the news "Steve Biko is dead" we were struck numb with disbelief. No, it can't be true! No, it must be a horrible nightmare and we will awake and find that really it is different—that Steve is alive even if it be in detention. But no, dear friends, he is dead and we are still numb with grief and groan with anguish, "Oh, God, where are you? Oh, God, do you really care? How can you let this happen to us?"

It all seems such a senseless waste of a wonderfully gifted person, struck down in the bloom of youth, a youthful bloom that some wanted to see blighted. What can be the purpose of such wanton destruction? God, do you really love us? What must we do which we have not done, what must we say which we have not said a thousand times over, oh, for so many years—that all we want is what belongs to all God's children, what belongs as an inalienable right: a place in the sun in our own beloved mother country. Oh, God, how long can we go on? How long can we go on appealing for a more just ordering of society where we all, black and white together, count not because of some accident of birth or a biological irrelevance, where all of us, black and white, count because we are human persons, human persons created in your own image.

In our grief and through our tears, we recall. Let us recall, my dear friends, that nearly two thousand years ago a young man was done to death and hung like a common criminal on a cross outside a city where they jeered at him and made fun of him. Let us recall how his followers were dejected and quite inconsolable in their grief. It all seemed so utterly meaningless, so utterly futile. . . .

We too . . . have been stunned by the death of another young man in his thirties. A young man completely dedicated to the pursuit of justice and righteousness, of peace and reconciliation. A young man completely committed to radical change in our beloved land. Even his worst enemies and detractors knew him as a person of utmost integrity and principle. And those who knew him better loved him as a warmhearted man with a huge sense of fun yet with a massive intellect. God called Steve to be his servant in South Africa, to speak up on behalf of God, declaring what the will of this God must be in a situation such as ours, a situation of evil and injustice, oppression, and exploitation.

God called him to be the founding father of the black consciousness movement, against which we have had tirades and fulminations. It is a movement by which God, through Steve, sought to awaken in the black person a sense of his intrinsic value and worth as a child of God, not needing to apologize for his existential condition as a black person, calling on blacks to glorify and praise God that he had created them black. Steve, with his brilliant mind that always saw to the heart of things, realized that until blacks asserted their humanity and their personhood, there was not the remotest chance for reconciliation in South Africa. . . . Steve knew and believed fervently that being pro-black was not the same thing as being anti-white. The black consciousness movement is not a "hate white movement" despite all you may have heard to the contrary. He had a far too profound respect for persons as persons to want them under ready-made, shop-soiled, second-hand categories.

I want again to appeal, with all the eloquence that I can muster, to our white fellow citizens and our white fellow Christians. We who today still advocate peaceful change and still talk about reconciliation and justice are in grave danger. The danger is that our credibility is being seriously eroded; for while we speak of peace and nonviolence we have the quite inexplicable action of the authorities in stopping those coming to mourn at Steve's funeral, an action that is most provocative. Why? We are answered by bulldozers which destroy the homes of squatters, leaving them without shelter in drenching rain. We thank God for the many whites who have shown compassion to these poor folk (and sheltered them on church property). We talk of nonviolence but we have the legalized violence that separates husband and father from his wife and family. We have long periods of detention without trial and deaths in detention. We have bannings and banishments.

I want to say, with all the circumspection and sense of responsibility that I can muster, that people can take only so much . . . I have seen too much violence to talk glibly about it, but I do want to issue a serious warning, a warning I am distressed to have to make . . . Please, please for God's sake listen to us while there is just a possibility of reasonably peaceful change. Nothing, not even the most sophisticated weapon, not even the most brutally efficient police, no, nothing will stop people once they are determined to achieve their freedom and their right to humanness. . . . For god's sake let us move away from the edge of the precipice. . . .

We weep with and pray for Ntsiki [Mrs. Biko] and all of Steve's family. We weep for ourselves. . . . Steve started something that is quite unstoppable. The powers of injustice, of oppression, of exploitation have done their worst and they have lost. . . . Many who support the present unjust system in this country know in their hearts that they are upholding a system that is evil and unjust and oppressive, and which is utterly abhorrent and displeasing to God. There is no doubt whatsoever that freedom is coming. Yes, it may be a costly struggle still. The darkest hour, they say, is before the dawn. We are experiencing the birth pangs of a new South Africa, a free South Africa, where all of us, black and white together will walk tall; where all of us, black and white together, will hold hands as we stride forth on the Freedom March to usher in the South Africa where people will matter because they are human beings made in the image of God.

We thank and praise God for giving us such a magnificent gift in Steve Biko . . .

SIX MURDERED CHILDREN
by Archbishop Desmond Tutu

On March 2, 1993, six children were brutally murdered in South Africa. Using automatic weapons, gunmen opened fire on a truck carrying twenty youngsters on their way to school. This eulogy was part of Archbishop Tutu's prayer during a pastoral visit to the site of the killings.

O God, we come to you . . . wondering what has happened to our people that anyone, for whatever reason, could mow down children in cold blood in this fashion. What could have got into those of your children to perform such a dastardly deed? We come here, Lord, asking you to drive away this evil as you drove out demons from those who were possessed, as you drove out death, as you triumphed on the Cross against all that was against your love, your compassion, and your caring.

Please, God, you have placed us in this land, such a beautiful land, a land which is so richly endowed with all of your gifts, a land that is being soaked so much with blood. Please, God, cleanse it, strengthen all of us to stand up against evil of every kind. Please, God, end this violence and bring to being this new dispensation when your children will be able to live in peace and harmony. . . .

God, we bring before you the families of those children who have been killed and those who have been injured. We ask you to give them the comfort of your Holy Spirit. We pray that we in a small way may be able to console and to comfort when we meet with some of them.

We pray also for those who have carried out this evil deed, for it does not matter how evil they are, they remain your children. We just pray that awareness of being your children will touch their hard hearts, make them repent, and stop them from ever being guilty of something of this kind again.

We pray for those who have been injured and we offer to you these children who have died. May their sacrifice ensure that freedom and peace will reign in this land. . . .

MARK SCHORER
by Alfred Kazin

Mark Schorer (1908–1977) was a novelist, literary critic, and biographer whose best-known work was his book on the life of Sinclair Lewis. He once wrote that "critics of literature have the same essential function as teachers of literature: this is not to direct the judgment of the audience, but to assist that audience in those disciplines of reading on which any meaningful judgment must rest." Schorer was dear friends with the writer, teacher, and critic Alfred Kazin, well known for his books **On Native Ground** *(1942),* **The Inmost Leaf** *(1955),* **Contemporaries** *(1960), and* **An American Procession** *(1984). Kazin gave his friend this final farewell.*

By the standards of the learned profession in which he spent so much of his life, my friend Mark Schorer was a success. He published several notable books in biography and criticism; he held all the leading fellowships bestowed by robber barons of the nineteenth century on docile professors in the twentieth; he taught at many leading universities, was sought after by Texas moneybags, was chairman of the notable English Department at Berkeley; he even published four books of fiction and over fifty stories.

But everyone who knew Mark and loved him, as I did, for his natural literary intelligence, his savviness, his stoicism, his ability and inability to hold in check his temperamental impatience and despair, knows that like so many interesting American writers Mark often regarded himself as a failure and was as vulnerable as he was charming, as anguished as he could be the life of the party.

Mark's last, posthumous, collection of stories, *Pieces of Life*, cleverly intersperses them with fragments of autobiography that say in every line, and especially between the lines, what

Whitman so proudly said of his visions—I am the man, I suffered, I was there.

Mark's most famous contribution to criticism was an essay, "Technique and Discovery." It was certainly technique, but something more than technique, that made Mark alternate his stories with autobiographical fragments. The stories belong to a certain old-fashioned *New Yorker* tradition of affluent pathos. There was a time, mostly in the 1950s, when the suffering conscience seemed to reside mostly under a Brooks Brothers tweed jacket. That style was overcome by the events of our perpetually torn world. So it was resourceful of Mark to intersperse his stories with fragments torn from his honest personal suffering.

It was for this desperate honesty, a certain candor, and openness of heart that he needed for the peace of his soul as well as for the task of describing so many writers and himself that I loved Mark. I learned from his literary intelligence; my wife and I had good reason to depend on his personal goodness and intellectual generosity to two writers. I loved him because, having to submit to many systems and institutions that are as hard on the writer's imaginative freedom as they are necessary to his appetite for knowledge and professional ambitions, Mark knew—how well he knew!—the gap between ourselves and the great shining world into which happiness escapes. Here in California I still look for him. I shall miss him to the end of my days.

MEDGAR EVERS
by Roy Wilkins

By the time Medgar Evers (1925–1963) was twenty-eight, he had been denied admission to the University of Mississippi Law School because he was black and had lost a family friend to a lynch mob. He began his work with the National Association for the Advancement of Colored People (NAACP), investigating racial killings. By 1963 he had become the most outspoken civil rights leader in Mississippi, demanding fair employment and integration. Along with several NAACP officials, Evers watched as President John Kennedy delivered a speech in response to two black students being prevented from entering the doors at the University of Alabama solely because of their race. Kennedy's strong remarks signaled the government's powerful support for civil rights.

Evers drove home, where his wife and three children were waiting for him. As he stepped out of his car, he was fatally shot in the back with a high-powered rifle. His friend and colleague Roy Wilkins spoke at the funeral, which was held on June 15 in Jackson, Mississippi. At the time of his death, his widow, Myrlie, said, "I am left without my husband and my children without a father, but I am left with strong determination to try to take up where he left off." Indeed she did. Today she is chairman emeritus of the NAACP.

There have been martyrs throughout history in every land and people in many high causes. We are here today in tribute to a martyr in the crusade for human liberty, a man struck down in mean and cowardly fashion by a bullet in the back.

The NAACP has had its share of sufferers. John R. Shillady, one of the earliest NAACP executive secretaries, who was badly beaten by a mob in Austin, Texas, in 1919; Elbert Williams, secretary of the Brownsville, Tennessee, NAACP, who was lynched in 1940; Rev. George W. Lee, officer of the Belzoni, Mississippi, NAACP, who registered to vote and was assassinated in 1955;

Harry T. Morre, NAACP state secretary for Florida, and his wife, both murdered in their beds in Miami, Florida, by a bomb on Christmas night, 1951.

Now in 1963, Medgar W. Evers, NAACP state secretary for Mississippi, shot June 12, 1963. . . . The lurking assassin at midnight June 11–12 pulled the trigger, but in all wars the men who do the shooting are trained and indoctrinated and keyed to action. The southern political system put him behind that rifle: the lily-white southern governments, local and state; the senators, governors, state legislators, mayors, judges, sheriffs, chiefs of police, commissioners, etc. Not content with mere disfranchisement, the officeholders have used unbridled political power to fabricate a maze of laws, customs, and economic practice which has imprisoned the Negro.

When at times it appeared that the rest of the nation might penetrate the Kingdom of Color, there were those ready always to beat back the adherents of decency and justice. Speaking of the public school decision of 1954 of the United States Supreme court, Senator James O. Eastland told a 1955 Sentobia, Mississippi, audience: "You are obligated to disobey such a court." . . . The killer must have felt that he had, if not an immunity, then certainly a protection for whatever he chose to do, no matter how dastardly.

Today as Americans and their president try to recover from their horror and to devise ways to correct the evils now so naked in our national life, these men in Congress, abetted by the timorous, the technical, and the selfishly ambitious, are raising the familiar—and by now the sickening—chorus of negations. With surgery required, they talk of ointments and pills. With speed the essence, they cite their rituals of procedure. Men may die and children may be stunted, but the seniority system and the filibuster rule must remain inviolate. . . .

. . . A southern state hires a retired professor to write a book setting forth the inferiority of the Negro race—twenty years after a Negro mathematician had helped in the calculations for the first atomic bomb! The opposition has been reduced to clubs, guns, hoses, dogs, garbage trucks, and hog wire compounds.

Obviously, the opposition is nearing bankruptcy. Fresh material is in short supply and strategy is stale and ineffective. Obviously, nothing can stop the drive for freedom. It will not cease here or elsewhere. After a hundred years of waiting and suffering, we are determined, in Baldwin language, not upon a bigger cage, but upon no cage at all.

Medgar Evers was the symbol of our victory and of their defeat.... In life he was a constant threat to the system, particularly in his great voter registration work. In the manner of his death, he was the victor over it. The bullet that tore away his life four days ago tore away at the system and helped to signal its end....

At his arrest with me two weeks ago today, Medgar found that the man in the fingerprint room was from his hometown, Decatur, Mississippi. There they were, the one hometown boy carrying out the routine of the old order, unaware, perhaps, that the other, calm and smiling, was the herald of that future day when no man, white or black, even in Mississippi, will be fingerprinted and photographed under a felony charge merely for seeking his manhood rights as an American citizen.

We in the NAACP loved him for himself, for his sincerity and integrity. We mourn him, but we are not cast down. For a little while he loaned us and his people the great strength of his body and the elixir of his spirit. We are grateful for this blessing. For him we shall all try harder to hold our nation to the concept of "all men." If he could live in Mississippi and not hate, so shall we, though we will ever stoutly contend for the kind of life his children and all others must enjoy in this rich land....

KARL MARX
by Friedrich Engels

On a rainy day at London's Highgate Cemetery, Karl Marx (1818–1883), the exiled revolutionary, the philosopher of the working class, and the co-author of **The Communist Manifesto,** *was laid to rest. He was buried alongside his wife, Jenny, whose death fifteen months earlier had devastated him. Although Marx himself was ill, a final emotional blow came when his eldest daughter, also named Jenny, died of bladder cancer at the age of thirty-eight. Marx's daughter Eleanor was the one to break the news to her father. She wrote, "I have lived many a sad hour, but none so bad as that. I felt that I was bringing my father his death sentence. I racked my brain all the long anxious day to find how I could break the news to him. But I did not need to, my face gave me away. Moor (Marx's nickname) said at once 'Our Jenny-chen is dead.' " The loss of his favorite daughter was too much for him to bear. Within several weeks he too would die.*

Marx's funeral was small; eight friends followed the coffin. His friend and collaborator Friedrich Engels, who went on to complete **Das Kapital,** *Socialism's bible, and supported Marx's projects and ideas until his own death, spoke these words over his friend's grave.*

On the fourteenth of March, at a quarter to three in the afternoon, the greatest living thinker ceased to think. He had been left alone for scarcely two minutes, and when we came back we found him in his armchair, peacefully gone to sleep—but forever.

An immeasurable loss has been sustained both by the militant proletariat of Europe and America, and by historical science, in the death of this man. The gap that has been left by the departure of this mighty spirit will soon enough make itself felt.

Just as Darwin discovered the law of development of organic nature, so Marx discovered the law of development of human history: the simple fact, hitherto concealed by an overgrowth of ideology, that mankind must first of all eat, drink, have shelter and clothing, before it can pursue politics, science, art, religion, etc. . . .

But that is not all. Marx also discovered the special law of motion governing the present-day capitalist mode of production and the bourgeois society that this mode of production has created. The discovery of surplus value suddenly threw light on the problem, in trying to solve [that] which all previous investigations, of both bourgeois economists and socialist critics, had been groping in the dark.

Two such discoveries would be enough for one lifetime. Happy the man to whom it is granted to make even one such discovery. But in every single field Marx investigated—and he investigated very many fields, none of them superficially—in every field, even in that of mathematics, he made independent discoveries.

Such was the man of science. But this was not even half the man. Science was for Marx a historically dynamic, revolutionary force. . . .

For Marx was before all else a revolutionist. His real mission in life was to contribute, in one way or another, to the overthrow of capitalist society and the state institutions which it had brought into being, to contribute to the liberation of the modern proletariat, which he was the first to make conscious of its own position and its needs, conscious of its conditions of emancipation. Fighting was his element. And he fought with a passion, a tenacity and a success such as few could rival. . . .

And consequently Marx was the best-hated and most calumniated man of his time. Governments, both absolutist and republican, deported him from their territories. Bourgeois, whether conservative or ultra-democratic, vied with one another in heaping slanders upon him. All this he brushed aside as though it were [a] cobweb, ignoring it, answering only when extreme necessity compelled him. And he died beloved, revered and mourned by millions of revolutionary fellow-workers—from the mines of Siberia to California, in all parts of Europe and America—and I make bold to say that though he may have had many opponents he had hardly one personal enemy.

His name will endure through the ages, and so also will his work.

LILLIAN HELLMAN
by William Styron

Lillian Hellman (1905–1984), the fiery, independent playwright and author, earned fame at the age of twenty-eight with her first play, **The Children's Hour** *(1934). She put that fame to work for progressive causes and gained more national acclaim than she had earned from her plays for refusing to cooperate with the Communist-hunting inquiry of the House Committee on Un-American Activities. In addition to her theater classics, including* **The Little Foxes** *(1939), Hellman is well remembered for her autobiographies:* **An Unfinished Woman** *(1969),* **Pentimento** *(1973), and* **Scoundrel Time** *(1975). She founded and headed a political organization, lectured widely on college campuses, fought her personal fights in public, and was a loyal friend to many. On July 3, 1984, eight eulogies were given at her graveside in Chilmark Cemetery on Martha's Vineyard. Writer and longtime friend William Styron spoke these words.*

I'm Bill Styron, an old friend of Lillian's, like many of us here. She once told me that this would be the day that I yearn for more than anything in my life, speaking words over her remains; and she cackled in glee. "Ha, ha," she said, and I cackled back. She said, "If you don't say utterly admiring and beautiful things about me, I'm going to cut you out of my will." I said there was no possible way that I could refrain from saying a few critical things, and she said, "Well, you're cut out already."

That was the way things went with us. I think we had more fights per man and woman contact than probably anyone alive. We were fighting all the time, and we loved each other a great deal for sure, because the vibrations were there. But our fights were never really, oddly enough, over abstract things like politics or philosophy or social dilemmas; they were always over such things as whether a Smithfield ham should be served hot or cold, or whether I had put too much salt in the black-eyed peas.

And I suddenly realized that this anger that spilled out from the lady, and it was almost a reservoir of anger, was really not directed at me or her other friends or even the black-eyed peas, but was directed at all the hateful things that she saw as menaces to the world. When she hated me and the ham, she was hating a pig like Roy Cohn, and I think this is what motivated her; and when one understood that the measure of her anger was really not personal but cosmic, then one was able to deal with her.

I was privileged . . . to be the last person to take her out to dinner; and I did so a few days ago here in Chilmark at La Grange. . . . We carved up a few mutually detested writers and one or two mediocre politicians and an elderly deceased novelist whom she specifically detested, and we got into this sort of thing; and we then started talking about her age.

. . . "I don't know whether the twentieth of June was my seventy-fourth or my seventy-third." And I measure this, because she had been doing this all her life, not as a vanity—though that was fine too, what's wrong with a little vanity—but as a kind of demonstration of the way that she was hanging on to life.

I suddenly realized as I was sitting there that she was painfully uncomfortable. She said she was cursed by God with having from birth a skinny ass; so I had to go and put things under her constantly, which was fine. She said this bolstered her skepticism of the existence of God. And I told her something that she had always responded to, that it was made up with an ample and seductive bosom, and she smiled at that. . . .

. . . I remember that gorgeous cackle of laughter which always erupted at moments when we were together with other people or alone and it was usually a cackle of laughter which followed some beautiful harpooning of a fraud or ninth-rater; and it was filled with a hatred, but it was usually hatred and anger which finally evolved into what I think she, like all of us, was searching for, some sort of transcendental idea which is love. And so, as we went out, I simply was in awe of this woman.

I had no final reflection except that perhaps she was in the end a lover, a mother, a sister, and a friend and in a strange way a lover of us all.

LILLIAN HELLMAN
by Jack Koontz

Jack Koontz, a Martha's Vineyard charter fishing boat captain, did not speak at the funeral but wrote these words in memory of her

Lillian Hellman was many things, and one of them was a fisherman. Some people love to fish or like to fish. Lillian placed no such verb between herself and fishing. She just fished. And she fished whenever she got the chance. If there is a patch of water where she is now, she is likely trying to coax a fish from it.

Lillian and I fished together for the first time six years ago. She and author John Hersey and I went out to Norman's Land and caught a box of bluefish. In the past she usually had a boat, she told me, and she wanted to own one again. I was not completely pleased with my boat at the time, so Lillian and I made a deal. Since fishing was difficult and even dangerous for her alone, and since she still wanted to fish, she would get a new boat and we would fish together. We fished every Saturday and the remaining days I used the boat for charter.

Lillian and I had many fine days on the waters around Martha's Vineyard over the past six years. Like any two fisherman, we had our ups and downs, but most of the time we got along pretty well, especially out on the water. She loved the water. Even when she was particularly ill and almost always uncomfortable, she relaxed when she went fishing. She never gave up on fishing. I suppose she was the sort of person who never gave up on anything she liked or cared about. . . .

The past two years, after her eyesight was nearly gone and walking without help became impossible, she decided to give the bluefish a break and, instead, to take on scup and flounder. I think she always liked bottom fishing better anyway, and she preferred to eat flounder. We would drift along the edge of Dog-fish Bar, picking up a fluke every ten or fifteen minutes, and the inevitable speedboat would pass a little too close. I made sure she was sitting secure in the seat so she wouldn't be knocked down by the wake and I warned her when it was about to rock our boat. She always did the same thing. She sat until the boat began to churn in the wake, then she got angry, grabbed the rail, stood up, and gave the guy the finger, hollering out that he had the whole ocean, so why did he have to bother us. Then we'd go back to fishing.

Last summer was tough for Lillian. She couldn't handle the rod by herself, her left side wasn't working so well then, and I held the rod steady for her while she cranked the scup or flounder to the surface. Then I'd hold the fish in front of her, so she could feel its size and shape. She usually caught the biggest fish. I don't know why, but she did. Perhaps it was because she had to work so hard to do it.

Not many people would have kept fishing as long as Lillian did. We were supposed to go fishing last Saturday, the day she died. She called me on Friday to check on the boat. She was anxious to get out on the water again.

Being on the ocean was good for Lillian these past few years and that she could still fish was important to her. She was angry about her failing health. When she fished she wasn't so angry.

She was a courageous woman. And she was a very good fisherman. I shall miss her.

JERRY GARCIA
by Robert Hunter

*Musical artist Jerry Garcia (1942–1995) was a founding member of
the band The Grateful Dead. His funeral took place on August 11,
1995, at St. Stephen's Church in Marin County, California. Two hundred and fifty friends, from what he called his extended family, came to
honor his memory. The service was conducted by Matthew Fox, the
Episcopalian preacher from Grace Cathedral in San Francisco. But
the high point was when his longtime song-writing partner, Robert
Hunter, rose and, reaching dramatically into the air, spoke these words.*

Jerry, my friend,
you've done it again,
even in your silence
the familiar pressure
comes to bear, demanding
I pull words from the air
with only this morning
and part of the afternoon
to compose an ode worthy
of one so particular
about every turn of phrase,
demanding it hit home
in a thousand ways
before making it his own,
and this I can't do alone.
Now that the singer is gone,
where shall I go for the song?

———————

Without your melody and taste
to lend an attitude of grace
a lyric is an orphan thing,

a hive with neither honey's taste
nor power to truly sting.

What choice have I but to dare and
call your muse who thought to rest
out of the thin blue air,
that out of the field of shared time,
a line or two might chance to shine—

As ever when we called,
in hope if not in words,
the muse descends.

How should she desert us now?
Scars of battle on her brow,
bedraggled feathers on her wings,
and yet she sings, she sings!

May she bear thee to thy rest,
the ancient bower of flowers
beyond the solitude of days,
the tyranny of hours—
the wreath of shining laurel lie
upon your shaggy head,
bestowing power to play the lyre
to legions of the dead.

If some part of that music
is heard in deepest dream,
or on some breeze of Summer
a snatch of golden theme,
we'll know you live inside us
with love that never parts
our good old Jack O'Diamonds
become the King of Hearts.

I feel your silent laughter
at sentiments so bold
that dare to step across the line
to tell what must be told,
so I'll just say I love you,
which I never said before
and let it go at that, old friend,
the rest you may ignore.

JACKIE ROBINSON
by Reverend Jesse Jackson

When baseball legend Jackie Robinson (1919–1972) signed a contract to play with the Brooklyn Dodgers in 1947, he broke the color bar in major league baseball. Despite his accession, Robinson endured harassment and insults from players, humiliations, such as being barred from staying at the same hotel as his white teammates, even death threats. His courageous response to such adversity made his success that much greater. He ended his first season as Rookie of the Year and in 1949 won the National League's coveted Most Valuable Player award. He played for ten seasons, helping the Dodgers win six pennants and a World Series. Robinson went on to a successful business career, and became deeply involved in the struggle for civil rights. Friends, family, and thousands more mourned his early death at the age of fifty-three. The funeral was held at the Riverside Church in New York City, after which Robinson's body was laid to rest at the Cypress Hill Cemetery in Queens next to his beloved son, Jackie, who had died the year before. Robinson's friend Reverend Jesse Jackson gave the eulogy.

Jackie's body was a temple of God, an instrument of peace that had no commitment to the idle gods of fame and materialism and empty awards and cheap trophies. . . . Jackie, as a figure in history, was a rock in the water, hitting concentric circles and ripples of new possibility. Jackie, as a co-partner with God, was a balm in Gilead, in America, in Ebbets Field. . . .

When Jackie took the field, something within us reminded us of our birthright to be free. And somebody without reminded us that it could be attained. There was strength and pride and power when the big rock hit the water, and concentric circles came forth and ripples of new possibility spread throughout this nation. . . .

He didn't integrate baseball for himself. He infiltrated baseball for all of us, seeking and looking for more oxygen for black survival, and looking for new possibility. . . . His feet on the baseball diamond made it more than a sport, a narrative of achievement more than a game. For many of us . . . it was a gift of new expectations. . . .

He helped us to ascend from misery, to hope, on the muscles of his arms and the meaning of his life. With Rachel, he made a covenant, where he realized that to live is to suffer, but to survive is to find meaning in that suffering. Today we can raise our hands and say Hallelujah. . . .

In his last dash, Jackie stole home. Pain, misery, and travail have lost. Jackie is saved. His enemies can leave him alone. His body will rest, but his spirit and his mind and his impact are perpetual and as affixed to human progress as are the stars in the heavens, the shine in the sun, and the glow in the moon. This mind, this mission, could not be held down by a grave. . . .

No grave can hold this body down. It belongs to the ages, and all of us are better off because the temple of God, the man with convictions, the man with a mission, passed this way.

MAHATMA MOHANDAS K. GANDHI
by Jawaharlal Nehru

At the age of seventy-eight Mahatma Mohandas K. Gandhi (1869–1948), the Indian spiritual leader who waged the eventually successful struggle against British Imperial rule, was fatally shot by a Hindu extremist as he walked with his granddaughters to an evening prayer meeting. Gandhi was killed as he greeted a colleague with the humble Hindu salute: his hands clasped and the points of his fingers brought to his chin.

When news of his death reached the people of India, hundreds of thousands of mourners grieved over the loss of this saintly man. Ironically, Gandhi was killed just after he had finished a five-day fast to encourage "communal friendship." His body was laid out on the second-floor balcony of his home, his head illuminated by a lamp with five candles, representing the five elements—air, water, light, earth, and fire. In orthodox Hindu fashion his body was carried from his New Delhi home on a simple wooden cot and covered with a white sheet. Afterward it was placed on a pyre and burned, the ashes scattered on the holy Jumna's waters. In a voice that quivered with emotion, Jawaharlal Nehru, the prime minister of India, gave Gandhi this farewell.

. . . A glory has departed and the sun that warmed and brightened our lives has set, and we shiver in the cold and dark. Yet he would not have us feel this way. After all, that glory that we saw for all these years, that man with the divine fire, changed us also—and such as we are, we have been molded by him during these years; and out of that divine fire many of us also took a small spark which strengthened and made us work to some extent on the lines that he fashioned. And so if we praise him, our words seem rather small, and if we praise him, to some extent we also praise ourselves. Great men and eminent men have monuments in bronze and marble set up for them, but this man of divine fire managed in his lifetime to become enshrined in millions and millions of hearts so that all of us became some-what of the stuff that he was made of, though to an infinitely lesser degree. He spread out in this way all over India, not in palaces only, or in select places or in assemblies, but in every hamlet and hut of the lowly and those who suffer. He lives in the hearts of millions and he will live for immemorial ages.

What, then, can we say about him, except to feel humble on this occasion? To praise him we are not worthy—to praise him whom we could not follow adequately and sufficiently. It is almost doing him an injustice just to pass him by with words when he demanded work and labor and sacrifice from us; in a large measure he made this country, during the last thirty years or more, attain to heights of sacrifice which in that particular domain have never been equaled elsewhere. He succeeded in that. Yet ultimately things happened which no doubt made him suffer tremendously, though his tender face never lost its smile and he never spoke a harsh word to anyone. Yet, he must have suffered—suffered for the failing of this generation whom he had trained, suffered because we went away from the path that he had shown us. And ultimately the hand of a child of his—for he, after all, is as much a child of his as any other Indian—the hand of a child of his struck him down.

. . . All we know is that there was a glory and that it is no more; all we know is that for the moment there is darkness, not so dark certainly, because when we look into our hearts we still find the living flame which he lighted there. And if those living flames exist, there will not be darkness in this land, and we shall be able, with our effort, remembering him and following his path, to illumine this land again, small as we are, but still with the fire that he instilled into us.

He was perhaps the greatest symbol of the India of the past, and, may I say, of the India of the future, that we could have had. We stand on this perilous edge of the present, between that past and the future to be, and we face all manner of perils. And the greatest peril is sometimes the lack of faith which comes to us, the sense of frustration that comes to us, the sinking of the heart and of the spirit that comes to us when we see ideals go overboard, when we see the great things that we talked about somehow pass into empty words, and life taking a different course. Yet, I do believe that perhaps this period will pass soon enough.

He has gone, and all over India there is a feeling of having been left desolate and forlorn. All of us sense that feeling, and I do not know when we shall be able to get rid of it. And yet together with that feeling there is also a feeling of proud thankfulness that it has been given to us of this generation to be associated with this mighty person. In ages to come, centuries and maybe millennia after us, people will think of this generation when this man of God trod on earth, and will think of us, who, however small, could also follow his path and tread the holy ground where his feet had been. Let us be worthy of him.

BENJAMIN FRANKLIN
by Mark Twain

Mark Twain wrote some of the most unorthodox essays of his time. He combined his wit and humor in quirky and philosophical pieces such as "How I Escaped Being Killed in a Duel" and "My First Lie and How I Got Out of It." He was a true nonconformist and in November 1880, after the Republicans celebrated the victory of their candidates in Hartford, Twain delivered his mock "Funeral Oration over the Grave of the Democratic Party." In 1870 Twain wrote this unusual and funny tribute to Benjamin Franklin (1706–1790), eighty years after Franklin's death. Here Twain honors Franklin by making fun of him. Leave it to Twain to tease one of history's most revered Americans.

Never put off till tomorrow what you can do day after tomorrow just as well.

This party was one of those persons whom they call Philosophers. He was twins, being born simultaneously in two different houses in the city of Boston. These houses remain unto this day, and have signs upon them worded in accordance with the facts. . . . The subject of this memoir was of a vicious disposition, and early prostituted his talents to the invention of maxims and aphorisms calculated to inflict suffering upon the rising generation of all subsequent ages. His simplest acts, also, were contrived with a view to their being held up for the emulation of boys forever—boys who might otherwise have been happy. It was in this spirit that he became the son of a soap-boiler, and probably for no other reason than that the efforts of all future boys who tried to be anything might be looked upon with suspicion unless they were the sons of soap-boilers. With a malevolence which is without parallel in history, he would work all day and then sit up nights and let on to be studying algebra by the light of a smoldering fire, so that all other boys might have to do that also or else have Benjamin Franklin thrown up to them. . . .

His maxims were full of animosity toward boys. Nowadays a boy cannot follow out a single natural instinct without tumbling over some of those everlasting aphorisms and hearing from Franklin on the spot. If he buys two cents worth of peanuts, his father says, "Remember what Franklin has said, my son, 'A groat a day's a penny a year' "; and the comfort is all gone out of those peanuts. If he wants to spin his top when he is done work, his father quotes, "Procrastination is the thief of time." If he does a virtuous action, he never gets anything for it, because "Virtue is its own reward." And that boy is hounded to death and robbed of his natural rest, because Franklin said once in one of his inspired flights of malignity—

Early to bed and early to rise
Make a man healthy and wealthy and wise.

As if it were any object to a boy to be healthy and wealthy and wise on such terms. The sorrow that that maxim has cost me through my parents' experimenting on me with it, tongue cannot tell. The legitimate result is my present state of general debility, indigence, and mental aberration. My parents used to have me up before nine o'clock in the morning, sometimes, when I was a boy. If they had let me take my natural rest, where would I have been now? Keeping store, no doubt and respected by all.

And what an adroit old adventurer the subject of this memoir was! In order to get a chance to fly his kite on Sunday, he used to hang a key on the string and let on to be fishing for lightning. And a guileless public would go home chirping about the "wisdom" and the "genius" of the hoary Sabbath-breaker. . . .

He invented a stove that would smoke your head off in four hours by the clock. One can see the almost devilish satisfaction he took in it, by his giving it his name.

He was always proud of telling how he entered Philadelphia,

for the first time, with nothing in the world but two shillings in his pocket and four rolls of bread under his arm. But really, when you come to examine it critically, it was nothing. Anybody could have done it. . . .

Benjamin Franklin did a great many notable things for his country, and made her young name to be honored in many lands as the mother of such a son. It is not the idea of this memoir to ignore that or cover it up. No; the simple idea of it is to snub those pretentious maxims of his, which he worked up with a great show of originality out of truisms that had become wearisome platitudes as early as the dispersion from Babel; and also to snub his stove . . . his unseemly endeavor to make himself conspicuous when he entered Philadelphia, and his flying his kite and fooling away his time in all sorts of such ways, when he ought to have been foraging for soap-fat or constructing candles.

I merely desired to do away with somewhat of the prevalent calamitous idea among heads of families that Franklin acquired his great genius by working for nothing, studying by moonlight, and getting up in the night instead of waiting till morning like a Christian, and that this programme, rigidly inflicted, will make a Franklin of every father's fool. It is time these gentlemen were finding out that these execrable eccentricities of instinct and conduct are only the evidences of genius, not the creators of it. I wish I had been the father of my parents long enough to make them comprehend this truth, and thus prepare them to let their son have an easier time of it. When I was a child I had to boil soap, notwithstanding my father was wealthy, and I had to get up early and study geometry at breakfast, and peddle my own poetry, and do everything just as Franklin did, in the solemn hope that I would be a Franklin some day. And here I am.

LEONARD BERNSTEIN
by Ned Rorem

Leonard Bernstein (1918–1990) was a most gifted and versatile American musician. His talent ranged from symphonic music to Broadway musicals and ballet to film and television. He composed several pieces for orchestra, including three symphonies, Facsimile, Fancy Free, and Kaddish, as well as innumerable chamber pieces and songs, and his West Side Story, On the Town, and Candide are theater classics. He also authored several books and was lauded for a series of televised concerts for children. At the age of forty he became the youngest music director ever engaged by the New York Philharmonic. On stage, as in life, Bernstein was demonstrative, often hugging and kissing fellow musicians after a particularly gratifying performance. His was an extravagant and unveiled life and the world seemed to know about and share in his personal joys and sorrows. Bernstein, who was a lifelong smoker, died of a heart attack brought on by progressive lung disease. His friend, fellow composer and essayist Ned Rorem, winner of the 1976 Pulitzer Prize in music, wrote this tender piece in his honor.

During the terrible hours after Leonard Bernstein's death, the press called repeatedly with irrelevant questions: How well did you know him? What made him so American? Did he smoke himself to death? Wasn't he too young to die? What was he really like? None of this seemed to matter since the world had suddenly grown empty—the most crucial musician of our time had vanished. But gradually it became clear that there are no irrelevant questions, and these were as good as any to set off a remembrance.

I was nineteen in early 1943, when we met in his West 52nd Street flat. Despite his show-biz personality he had, and forever retained, a biblical look, handsome and nervy as the shepherd David who would soon be king and psalmodized throughout his days. To me, a Midwest Quaker, his aura was Jewish and quite glamorous, while to him I remained always something of a reticent WASP who never quite got the point.

How well did I know him? To "know well" has to do with intensity more than with habit. Everyone in Lenny's vast entourage thought himself to be, at one time or another, the sole love of his life, and I was no exception. The fact that he not only championed my music, but conducted it in a manner coinciding with my very heartbeat, was naturally not unrelated to the love. Years could pass without our meeting, then for weeks we'd be inseparable. During those periods he would play as hard as he worked with a power of concentration as acute for passion as for Passions.

In Milan, in 1954, when he was preparing *La Sonnambula* for La Scala I asked him how Callas was to deal with. "Well, she knows what she wants and gets it," he said, "but since she's always right, this wastes no time. She's never temperamental or unkind during rehearsal—she saves that for parties." Lenny was the same: socially exasperating, even cruel with his manipulative narcissism (but only with peers, not with unprotected underlings), generous with his professional sanctioning of what he believed in.

Was he indeed so American? He was the sum of his contradictions. His most significant identity was that of jack-of-all-trades (which the French aptly call *l'homme orchestre*), surely a European trait, while Americans have always been specialists. If he did want desperately to create a self-perpetuating American art, his own music, even the Broadway scores, was a grab bag of every imaginable foreign influence. Night after smoke-filled night we could sit up arguing the point, for Lenny ached to be taken seriously as a sage. Nothing was ever resolved, of course, not so much because musical philosophy is an impotent pursuit, as because he was less a thinker than a doer. Yes, he was frustrated at forever being "accused" of spreading himself thin, but this very spreading, like the frustration itself, defined his theatrical nature. Had he concentrated on but one of his gifts, that gift would have shriveled.

I last saw Lenny in May, when, with two other people, we went to a dance program, afterward to a restaurant. His role, as always, was to be the life of the party, but repartee fell flat, the concerned pronouncements were incomplete, his breath distressingly short, and he disappeared like a ghost in the midst of the meal. A month later we spoke on the phone, not about health or music, but about the plight of a young Romanian student without a passport. Lenny could simultaneously focus on his navel and on the universe, even in his agony.

Was he too young to die? What is too young? Lenny led four lives in one, so he was not seventy-two, but two hundred and eighty-eight. Was he, as so many have meanly claimed, paying for the rough life he led? As he lived many lives, so he died many deaths. Choking may have been one cause, but so was overwork, and especially sorrow at a world he so longed to change but which remained as philistine and foolish as before. Which may ultimately be the broken-hearted reason any artist dies. Or any person.

So what was he really like? Lenny was like everyone else only more so, but nobody else was like him.

GEORGE BALANCHINE
by Arthur Gold and Robert Fizdale

Russian-born George Balanchine (1904–1983) was one of the finest choreographers in the history of ballet. His influence revitalized the appeal of the art and inspired and nurtured generations of talented dancers. Balanchine emigrated to the United States in 1933 when he accepted an offer to co-found both a company (the New York City Ballet) and a school (the School of American Ballet). Balanchine broke from tradition by creating his own new works rather than reviving old classics. He left over two hundred ballets, including **Apollo**, **Serenade**, **The Prodigal Son**, **The Nutcracker**, *and* **Don Quixote**. *Athough often thought of as detached, Balanchine had a full emotional life. He was married four times, each time to a dancer for whom he created ballets. Balanchine's very close friends, duo pianists Arthur Gold and Robert Fizdale, wrote this in his honor.*

George Balanchine liked to say, quoting Mayakovsky, "I am not a man, but a cloud in trousers." And now, the luminous cloud has floated off, leaving us with a loss far deeper than the grave. Balanchine spoke for all of us. Diffident as he was in private life, in his ballets he shared his daydreams, his joys, his troubled loves, his fears, his instinct for elegance and order, and his passion for youth with those who admired his work. He has been a poet for poets, a musician for musicians, and a dramatist for anyone who wishes to understand the human heart. Reality for him was the stage and he gave us stylized visions that seem truer than life. His genius was multilingual. A couple in love walk slowly onto a twilit stage, music of Fauré is heard, and the perfume of French poetry lies lightly in air. *The Four Temperaments* and *Kammermusik* speak perfect German. *Agon*—cool, sarcastic, analytic, probing—is Sixties America. Stravinsky said that when he first saw *Movements for Piano and Orchestra*, "George shows me things in my own music that I didn't realize were there."

W. H. Auden said of Balanchine, "He's not an intellectual, he's something deeper, a man who understands everything." And indeed, he has given us a history of manners, music, and the dance, as seen by a twentieth-century master. Through his eyes we saw gods and mythical creatures move in limitless space. . . . Ballanchine's genius is unclassifiable. . . .

Balanchine's genius in dance innovation was limitless. His revolutionary use of the elements of ballet—speed, balances, steps, lifts, gestures, partnering—made us see anew. As with Mozart, his inventions came to us as inevitable extensions of his art. Creation was his life, inventiveness his toy. He could transform everyday life into an unexpected fete.

"We'll be late for theater," we said one evening after an early dinner. "Let's find a taxi." "No, no," he said, "subway much better." And like a mythical guide he made the dingy steps, the sinister train, the underground arrival at the State Theater a Tiepoloesque flight into heaven. Ordinary life seemed not to exist for George. Olympian in his simplicity, he cooked his Russian food, he ironed his own shirts, he planted flowers and trees, he trained his cat to jump—all with the concentration, the dispatch, the single-mindedness that he gave to his choreography.

If his work gave him trouble no one was aware of it. A religious believer, he trusted the immense talent God had given him. Balanchine never tried consciously to create a masterpiece. He made masterpieces by combining his unique knowledge of the dance and a profound emotional instinct with an absolute honesty about the music he was working with. His nose would quiver with characteristic disdain at the word "inspiration." But how he inspired others! . . .

We who have known Balanchine for almost forty years never failed . . . to ask his musical advice. The essentials—rhythm, tempo, phrasing, and structure—were what he spoke of. Whenever expressiveness was mentioned he would say, "That you find in the music." Then with his enigmatic smile he would add, "And if you're lucky, in here," pointing to his heart. . . .

DIANA, PRINCESS OF WALES
by Earl Spencer

Few events have engendered such worldwide attention as the death of Diana, the Princess of Wales (1961–1997). Adored by millions, Diana represented a fresh and vibrant addition to England's reserved royal family. The British public supported her even as her unhappy marriage to Prince Charles ended. Tragically she was killed in a car accident at the age of thirty-six. The press had shadowed and hounded Diana since she had become part of the monarchy in 1981. As she was chauffeured in a car on the night of her death, paparazzi photographers engaged her driver in a chase, many believe, causing the accident and her untimely death. Her funeral at Westminster Abbey was attended by millions. Following her casket through the streets of London were her sons, William and Harry, Prince Charles, Prince Philip, and her brother, Earl Spencer, who gave the eulogy at her funeral. Diana's body was laid to rest on the island at the Round Oval, an ornamental lake within Althorp, the Spencer family estate, in England.

I stand before you today, the representative of a family in grief in a country in mourning before a world in shock. We are all united not only in our desire to pay our respects to Diana but rather in our need to do so.

For such was her extraordinary appeal that the tens of millions of people taking part in this service all over the world via television and radio who never actually met her feel that they too lost someone close to them in the early hours of Sunday morning. It is a more remarkable tribute to Diana than I can ever hope to offer her today.

Diana was the very essence of compassion, of duty, of style, of beauty. All over the world she was a symbol of selfless humanity. All over the world, a standard bearer for the rights of the truly downtrodden, a very British girl who transcended nationality. Someone with a natural nobility who was classless and who proved in the last year that she needed no royal title to continue to generate her particular brand of magic.

Today is our chance to say thank you for the way you brightened our lives, even though God granted you but half a life. We will all feel cheated always that you were taken from us so young and yet we must learn to be grateful that you came along at all. Only now that you are gone do we truly appreciate what we are now without, and we want you to know that life without you is very, very difficult. . . .

There is a temptation to rush to canonize your memory; there is no need to do so. You stand tall enough as a human being of unique qualities not to need to be seen as a saint. Indeed to sanctify your memory would be to miss out on the very core of your being, your wonderfully mischievous sense of humor with a laugh that bent you double.

Your joy for life, transmitted wherever you took your smile, and the sparkle in those unforgettable eyes. Your boundless energy, which you could barely contain. But your greatest gift was your intuition and it was a gift you used wisely. This is what underpinned all your other wonderful attributes and if we look to analyze what it was about you that had such a wide appeal, we find it in your instinctive feel for what was really important in all our lives. . . .

Diana explained to me once that it was her innermost feelings of suffering that made it possible for her to connect with her constituency of the rejected. And here we come to another truth about her. For all the status, the glamour, the applause, Diana remained throughout a very insecure person at heart, almost childlike in her desire to do good for others. . . .

The last time I saw Diana was on July 1, her birthday, in London, when typically she was not taking time to celebrate her special day with friends but was guest of honor at a special charity fund-raising evening. She sparkled of course, but I would rather cherish the days I spent with her in March when she came to visit me and my children in our home in South Africa. I am proud of the fact that apart from when she was on display meeting President Mandela we managed to contrive to stop the ever-present paparazzi from getting a single picture of her—that meant a lot to her.

These were days I will always treasure. It was as if we had been transported back to our childhood when we spent such an enormous amount of time together—the two youngest in the family. Fundamentally she had not changed at all from the big sister who mothered me as a baby, fought with me at school, and endured those long train journeys between our parents' homes with me at weekends. It is a tribute to her level-headedness and strength that despite the most bizarre-like life imaginable after her childhood, she remained intact, true to herself.

There is no doubt that she was looking for a new direction in her life at this time. She talked endlessly of getting away from England, mainly because of the treatment that she received at the hands of the newspapers. I don't think she ever understood why her genuinely good intentions were sneered at by the media, why there appeared to be a permanent quest on their behalf to bring her down. It is baffling.

My own and only explanation is that genuine goodness is threatening to those at the opposite end of the moral spectrum. It is a point to remember that of all the ironies about Diana, perhaps the greatest was this—a girl given the name of the ancient goddess of hunting was, in the end, the most hunted person of the modern age.

She would want us today to pledge ourselves to protecting her beloved boys, William and Harry, from a similar fate and I do this here, Diana, on your behalf. We will not allow them to suffer the anguish that used regularly to drive you to tearful despair. And beyond that, on behalf of your mother and sisters, I pledge that we, your blood family, will do all we can to continue the imaginative and loving way in which you were steering these two exceptional young men so that their souls are not simply immersed in duty and tradition, but can sing openly as you planned.

We fully respect the heritage into which they have both been born and will always respect and encourage them in their royal role. But we, like you, recognize the need for them to experience as many different aspects of life as possible to arm them spiritually and emotionally for the years ahead. I know you would have expected nothing less from us.

William and Harry, we all care desperately for you today. We are all chewed up with the sadness at the loss of a woman who was not even our mother. How great your suffering is, we cannot even imagine.

I would like to end by thanking God for the small mercies he has shown us at this dreadful time. For taking Diana at her most beautiful and radiant and when she had joy in her private life. Above all we give thanks for the life of a woman I am so proud to be able to call my sister—the unique, the complex, the extraordinary, and irreplaceable Diana, whose beauty, both internal and external, will never be extinguished from our minds.

WILLIAM EDGETT SMITH
by Calvin Trillin

William Edgett Smith (1930–1992) was a foreign correspondent and writer for Time *magazine. He met humorist and fellow writer Calvin Trillin in 1961 at the New York bureau of* Time. *The two men and their families became very close and Smith bestowed upon Trillin the honor of becoming the godfather of his daughter, Caroline. When Smith died at the age of sixty-two, the funeral was held at the First Presbyterian Church in New York City's Greenwich Village. Trillin gave this eulogy for his longtime friend.*

In Bill Smith's junior high school in California, all boys were required to attend a series of lectures on gentlemanly comportment given by a vice principal who worked for the Park Service in the summer and who Bill always referred to as Ranger-Naturalist Floyd Brown. One of Ranger-Naturalist Floyd Brown's rules was that in crossing the street in the company of a lady a gentleman *always* walks between the lady and the approaching traffic. When Bill first told us that, I pointed out that a strict interpretation of the rule meant that in crossing a two-way street, a gentleman had to switch sides in the middle.

"Absolutely," Bill said. "In fact, Ranger-Naturalist Floyd Brown always made that point by asking a question that he answered himself. 'Does the rules mean that you must change sides in the middle of the street?' he'd ask. '*Yes, it does.*'"

When we had this conversation, maybe forty years after Ranger-Naturalist Floyd Brown's lecture, Bill was still observing the rule about how a gentleman crosses the street in the company of a lady. There were still a few two-way streets in Greenwich Village then, and I found it somehow comforting that tourists who observed a tall man suddenly jump to the other side of his partner while crossing, say, University Place, might think they were witnessing yet another demonstration of bizarre Village behavior when, in fact, they were seeing Bill Smith follow the rules of gentlemanly comportment as laid down by Ranger-Naturalist Floyd Brown in Glendale, California, in 1940.

Bill was not one to place a time limit on commitments, and one of his commitments was to gentlemanly comportment. Although his interpretation of gentlemanly comportment went a lot further than the niceties taught by Ranger-Naturalist Floyd Brown, it started with that sort of thing. He held open doors. He put people at their ease. When you had dinner with him, you had to watch him toward the end of the meal, because he'd wander off from the table and it would later turn out that he hadn't wandered to the telephone or restroom but had quietly settled the check. In conversation with him, you had to be careful about mentioning anything you might be interested in having—an article from the late fifties that seemed impossible to find or book you always wanted to read—because a few days later you'd discover that it had been slipped through the mail slot. He listened to people when they talked. If the person talking to him was shorter than he was, which most people were, he'd sometimes stand in an awkward-looking spread-eagled position so the other person wouldn't have to look up. That was gentlemanly comportment.

He had a no-time-limit commitment to places—Glendale or the Seychelles or Half Moon Bay or Bali—although, despite all the traveling he had done, he remained suspicious of flying. When he first went to Africa, I got a postcard from him that said, in its entirety, "Thirty-six takeoffs, thirty-six landings."

He preferred driving. In fact, he adored driving. More than once, I discovered that, although he had been able to get away from the city for only a day and Caroline and Genny hadn't been able to get away at all, he had gone up to his house in New Hampshire—requiring a round trip drive of about nine hours.

"I guess you had some pretty important business up there," I'd say.

"Well," he'd say, "You never want to let the lawn go in a place like that." ...

And he had a commitment to people that was without time limit. Genny and Caroline, of course. But he remained friends with an astonishing array of people. The Smith house on Charles Street had the steadiest stream of houseguests in the Village. Once I raised with Genny the possibility that someone had simply scrawled Bill's name and number on the wall of an airport in Frankfurt or Hong Kong as an easy touch for anyone going to New York. But she said he seemed to know these people. He had lunched with them regularly in the coffee shop of the Akbar Hotel in New Delhi or visited their farm when there was still a place called Rhodesia or sat next to them during the lectures of Ranger-Naturalist Floyd Brown.

And he had a no-time-limit commitment to decency and integrity and trustworthiness that was so much a part of him that he didn't even recognize it. A wise woman our family knew—someone who was brilliant and accomplished and might have been expected to divide up the world according to brilliance and accomplishment—used to say that the world was divided between people who could be trusted to do what they said they'd do, and everyone else. I eventually decided that she was right, and that there were about eleven of the first kind of people. Now there are ten.

Every family has shorthand ways of talking, and in our family Bill was the shorthand for that automatic commitment to decency and integrity and trustworthiness. When we found ourselves trying to explain to our girls what we found wrong with the way some grown-up had behaved, we often said, "Try to think of what Bill would have done in that situation."

And that seems to me part of his legacy. All of us can ask ourselves at any time, "What would Bill do in this situation?" Then we can do it.

JIM HENSON
by Frank Oz

Few children in the world cannot identify Big Bird, Ernie and Burt,
and Kermit the Frog, Jim Henson's (1936–1990) Muppet characters
from **Sesame Street**. *When Henson died, his friends, collaborators,*
and family chose to celebrate his life. Two memorial services were held,
one at New York's Cathedral of St. John the Divine and the other at
London's St. Paul's Cathedral, and both were packed with admirers.
Jim Henson had asked that there be a jazz band at his funeral and that
no one wear black. In New York, the band played "When the Saints
Come Marching In" and the church was filled with colorful costumes
and hundreds of butterflies made in the Henson workshop. Most touch-
ing were the letters that poured by the sackful into the production
company's Manhattan headquarters from people all over the world,
especially children. One read: "I wish you did not die. I love you a lot."
Frank Oz, Jim Henson's longtime friend and co-worker, who is the
well-known feature film director and the performer who continues to
bring Miss Piggy to life, gave this eulogy at the service in London.

. . . After the service in New York . . . I wandered around for
days and weeks like many of us did. And, while I worked, and
while I was with my family, I thought about Jim. I couldn't help
but think about Jim.

I thought of course about what an insane, profound loss it
was. And then of course so many images and memories of Jim
came back to me. So many images. But one image kept coming
back to me—just a fleeting moment. And it was not of Jim per-
forming or directing. It was not of Jim with his family. It was not
of Jim with his colleagues. And it was not Jim working so hard.
And it was not even of the great, stupid, silly fun that we all had
with Jim—that I had with Jim.

But this one image kept coming back to me . . . Just of Jim, standing, with his arms folded, just having a very warm smile—looking. And, it wouldn't go away. It just kept on coming back. I realized it was Jim, appreciating. I know where I got that image from, I think. It was from the *Muppet Show* here at ATV or *The Dark Crystal*, the movie, or wherever we were shooting when we would look back at the playbacks. The television monitor would be right there. We would shoot the movie or shoot the performance, as many of you know. And then we would play it back and judge it. Often we would judge it and say, "Oh, that was terrible. Let's do it again." But so many times I would see Jim—just appreciating it.

Many people see Jim as an extraordinary creator. I realize that I see Jim first as an appreciator. He appreciated so much. He loved London. He loved walking on the Heath. He loved . . . Parliament Hill, flying kites. He appreciated it so much. He appreciated his family and his colleagues and his Muppet family. And he appreciated the performances and design of a puppet. He appreciated the art objects that he might buy. He appreciated the detail in a Persian rug. He appreciated . . . just beauty.

Many times we would have meetings. I've known Jim for twenty-seven years now and this would always happen. And I'm sure some of you will remember. We would have a meeting and if it was a pretty day outside, he'd say, "Gee, couldn't we go outside? Couldn't we? It's nice out there. Couldn't we just go outside? Why sit in here?"

And he appreciated the day. He didn't realize why . . . why sit in a stuffy room when you could appreciate beauty out there? And I remember when we had meetings he would . . . often say, "Gee, can't we eat? Why don't we—I mean—isn't it time to eat? Can't we eat while we meet?"

And it wasn't because he was hungry. He just . . . it was a time to appreciate eating and it was a time to appreciate working. And even when he ate, I remember, he would always take dessert. He loved dessert. And he would . . . I just have this image of him . . . when you brought the tray over, I remember him saying, "What—what's that thingy—there?" He was always wiggling his finger and saying, "What's that little dessert thing?" I don't know why, but he couldn't order dessert without wiggling his finger. I'm not quite sure why that is but then he'd say, "I'll, I'll take that, that thingy there." And he would have it. And then he would eat it. And when he was eating it, you'd hear these little "Mmm's" from him, as he ate the dessert. "Mmmm. Mmmm."

And it wasn't just that it tasted good, which it did. But it was the time at that moment to appreciate it. To appreciate where he was at that moment—eating that dessert. And I think life was just this dessert for him. I really don't believe that Jim could have been such an extraordinary creator if he hadn't been such an extraordinary appreciator. . . .

II. Letters

MAJOR SULLIVAN BALLOU
to Sarah Ballou

Civil War hero Major Sullivan Ballou (1827–1861) wrote his last let-
ter while at Camp Clark, outside Washington, D.C. There he waited for
orders that would take him and twenty-seven of his men to their deaths
at the Battle of Bull Run. Ballou had lost his father at a young age and
grew up in poverty. But he persevered and went on to become a lawyer
and a well-liked member of the Rhode Island House of Representatives.
He did not have to go to war but, as a man of principle, volunteered
because of his ardent support of Lincoln. He died in hand-to-hand com-
bat at the age of thirty-four, leaving his wife, Sarah, and their two boys,
Edgar and Willie. Sarah, who was widowed at twenty-five, never mar-
ried again.

July 14, 1861

My very dear wife,
    The indications are very strong that we shall move in a few
days—perhaps tomorrow. Lest I should not be able to write
again, I feel impelled to write a few lines that may fall under
your eye when I shall be no more.
    . . . I have no misgivings about, or lack of confidence in, the
cause in which I am engaged, and my courage does not halt or
falter. I know how strongly American Civilization now leans on
the triumph of the Government, and how great a debt we owe to
those who went before us through the blood and sufferings of
the Revolution. And I am willing—perfectly willing—to lay
down all my joys in this life to help maintain the Government,
and to pay that debt. . . .
    Sarah my love for you is deathless; it seems to bind me with
mighty cables that nothing but Omnipotence could break; and
yet my love of Country comes over me like a strong wind and
bears me irresistibly on with all these chains to the battlefield.

The memories of the blissful moments I have spent with you come creeping over me, and I feel most deeply gratified to God and to you that I have enjoyed them so long. And how hard it is for me to give them up and burn to ashes the hopes of future years, when, God willing, we might still have lived and loved together, and seen our boys grow up to honorable manhood around us. I have, I know, but few and small claims upon Divine Providence, but something whispers to me—perhaps it is the wafted prayer of my little Edgar, that I shall return to my loved ones unharmed. If I do not my dear Sarah, never forget how much I loved you, and when my last breath escapes me on the battlefield, it will whisper your name.

Forgive my many faults, and the many pains I have caused you. How thoughtless and foolish I have often times been! How gladly would I wash out with my tears every little spot upon your happiness, and struggle with all the misfortunes of this world to shield you and my children from harm. But I cannot. I must watch you from the spirit world and hover near you, while you buffet the storms with your precious little freight, and wait with sad patience till we meet to part no more.

But O Sarah! if the dead can come back to this earth and flit unseen around those they love, I shall always be near you; in the brightest day and the darkest night . . . always, always, and if there be a soft breeze upon your cheek, it will be my breath, as the cool air fans your throbbing temple, it shall be my spirit passing by.

Sarah, do not mourn me dead; think I am gone and wait for thee, for we shall meet again. . . .

Sullivan

BENJAMIN FRANKLIN
to Elizabeth Hubbard

Benjamin Franklin's (1706–1790) drive to master different fields of endeavor seemed unquenchable as he became a successful printer and publisher, inventor, writer, and philosopher. An accomplished diplomat and statesman, he was among those who signed both the Declaration of Independence and the Constitution of the United States. His belief in rational thinking and letting nature serve man is well reflected in this letter, which he wrote to Elizabeth Hubbard, the stepdaughter of his favorite brother, John, who had died of bladder disease. Franklin's words have been echoed many times since the eighteenth century, giving great comfort to mourners.

February 22, 1756

Dear Child,

I condole with you; we have lost a most dear and valuable relation, but it is the will of God and Nature that these mortal bodies be laid aside, when the soul is to enter into real life; 'tis rather an embryo state, a preparation for living; a man is not completely born until he be dead. Why then should we grieve that a new child is born among the immortals? A new member added to their happy society? We are spirits. That bodies should be lent us, while they can afford us pleasure, assist us in acquiring knowledge, or doing good to our fellow creatures, is a kind and benevolent act of God—when they become unfit for these purposes and afford us pain instead of pleasure—instead of an aid, become an encumbrance and answer none of the intentions for which they were given, it is equally kind and benevolent that a way is provided by which we may get rid of them. Death is that way. We ourselves prudently choose a partial death. In some cases a mangled painful limb, which cannot be restored, we willingly cut off. He who plucks out a tooth, parts with it freely since the pain goes with it, and he that quits the whole body, parts at once with all pains and possibilities of pains and diseases it was liable to, or capable of making him suffer.

Our friend and we are invited abroad on a party of pleasure—that is to last forever—His chair was first ready and he is gone before us—we could not all conveniently start together, and why should you and I be grieved at this, since we are soon to follow, and we know where to find him. Adieu

HORACE GREELEY
to Margaret Fuller

Horace Greeley (1811–1872) was the founding editor of the **New York Tribune***, one of America's first penny daily papers. He was also an author and a politician, whose ideas and work had a significant influence on events during the Civil War. Greeley was known for his scathing exposure of legislative abuses, and he expressed his vehement stand against slavery in a well-publicized letter to Lincoln entitled "The Prayer of Twenty Million." On the personal front Greeley suffered many losses; of his seven children, only two survived past their fifth year. The most tragic moment in his life was the death of his son Arthur, also known as Pickie, who died of cholera at the age of five. Greeley was devastated over the child's death and wrote to his friend Margaret Fuller, the American writer, editor, and critic, who was at that time in Rome, serving as the* **Tribune***'s European correspondent. About the letter she said, "I have shed rivers of tears over the inexpressibly affecting letter . . . the image of Pickie's little dancing figure, lying still and stark, had made me weep more than all else."*

Coney Island Beach,
near New York
July 23, 1849

Ah Margaret! the world grows dark with us. You grieve, for Rome has fallen; I mourn, for Pickie is dead! The one sunburst of joy that has gladdened my rugged pathway has departed, and henceforth life must be heavy and rayless. I have never had an intimate friend—my life has been too intensely busy and my aims not entirely common; but this one dear being already promised to be my friend in every trial, my solace in every care. To him my form and features were the standard of beauty, and even my singing was music. He was my one auditor who never tired—my companion on whom my leisure hour was ever spent and never wasted. I had no hope, no dream of personal good or distinction of which his delight, his advantage, was not the better part; and now he is dead! Ah! my friend! did I not realize that my Father in Heaven has dealt this terrible blow not merely to punish my sins but to wean me from sordid ways and low aspirations to purity and Him, I should indeed be most wretched. But I know He doeth all things well, and will strive to be resigned. Nay, I think I am.

You have spent years in Europe and reveled amid the treasures of Art and Genius that Rome encloses. I have known Pickie meantime and would not exchange with you. You knew something of him in his infancy, but . . . he was five last March— a tall, fair, glorious boy, his golden locks uncut, his grace, wit and even wisdom surpassing all you can imagine. Some of his observations were really keen and searching . . . he was generous and tender-hearted, and always laying by or begging some coin to give to the poor. O he was a dear child, and it is very hard to leave him in the cold earth and go back to struggling with the means for ends which seem too like them.

We had not the least premonition of this blow. I last saw him in health at 10 A.M. on the 11th, when I went downtown leaving him as hearty and joyous as ever in the world. . . . Very soon he was vomiting as well as purging. . . . We doctored incessantly . . . but our doctor was called away at 8 by a sudden and dangerous illness of his own wife; he did not return until after 12, and meantime (perhaps through mismanagement) the reaction had been lost and our darling had for two or three hours been sinking; we went to work desperately, but the only effect was to torture him; at 2 he was hopelessly sinking. . . . He had struggled with superhuman strength all day to throw off the clothes that we held upon him, trying to produce perspiration . . . even biting the fingers by which we were holding him down under the clothes, and constantly struggling to get up in the bed; and at last the inflammation in his stomach striking to his brain he struggled up on end repeatedly, exclaiming at intervals,—"O it's no use trying to do any thing for me! . . . I am afraid! . . . I am sinking! . . . I am dying . . ." He then sank down in the bed, and offered no more resistance to whatever we chose to do. . . . The next day his cold ashes rode between his father and mother to Greenwood, as his sister's had done two years before. I carried the new coffin down into our vault and laid it beside the other— the mother going down into the narrow house and directing, with a burning heart but a tearless face. Ah me! Ah me!

Mother has been well and strong throughout, though you know that, compared with him, all the world beside was nothing to her. The next day we were compelled to begin (or rather resume) a struggle for the life of our last remaining child, now eight months old, whom Malaria, Teething, Diarrhea and finally Sprue came very near carrying off. . . . This is a sad letter for us. . . .

Yours, Horace Greeley

MARSILIO FICINO
to Bernardo Bembo

Marsilio Ficino (1433–1499) was a priest, philosopher, and the head of the Platonic Academy of Florence, who translated the works of Plato, Plotinus, and other ancient thinkers. Like Pythagoras, he was a strict vegetarian, who rose with the sun and led a life of abstinence and chastity. He lived in early Renaissance in Florence and corresponded with distinguished individuals from prominent Florentine families, as well as with cardinals, ambassadors, philosophers, and scholars of literature and learning. Here he consoles his friend Bernardo Bembo, a Venetian statesman and orator, during a time of grief. Who exactly Bembo is mourning is unknown. The letter was written sometime between 1470 and 1476.

Tell me, Bernardo, what is it that you mourn in a friend's death? Is it death? Or is it the person who is dead? If it is death, mourn your own, Bernardo. For as surely as he is dead will you too die; or rather, you are dying; for from moment to moment your past life is dying. If it is the dead person you mourn, is it because he was bad, or because he was good? If he was bad, you are well rid of such a companion; and you should not grieve over your blessings. If he was good, which I prefer to think since he is loved by a good and prudent man, surely for him it is good to live removed from the continuous death of the body. It is not right to grudge a friend such great blessings. Perhaps you grieve because you no longer see him anywhere as you used to. However, was not this man your friend in that he loved you? Now what was it that loved you? Was it not the soul itself, the soul which also knew you? But you saw his soul no differently then than now; and you see it now no less than then.

You will perhaps complain of his absence. But, as souls do not fill space, they become present not in any particular place but in thought. When you do not consider him you cannot be sad. But when you do consider him, which you do as you please, you at once recall his presence. You should never complain about his absence then, unless perhaps you object that it is not the way of the free soul to commune with the one now imprisoned in your body. Separate the mind from the body, Bernardo, if you can, and, believe me, your souls will quickly meet. But if you cannot do this, do not doubt they will meet a little later whether you will or not. For if we compare our life to our will, it is exceedingly brief; if we compare it to the age of the world, it is but an instant; and, compared to the age of God, even less than an instant.

Farewell, and live in God, since He alone is eternal life. He alone drives death and the sorrow of death far from His worshippers.

JULIUS ROSENBERG
to Manny Bloch

At the height of American anti-Communist hysteria during the late 1940s and early 1950s, Julius Rosenberg (1918–1953) and his wife, Ethel (1915–1953), were arrested on a charge of conspiracy to transmit atomic secrets to the Soviet Union. The key witnesses for the prosecution were David and Ruth Greenglass, Ethel's younger brother and sister-in-law, who were named co-conspirators in the indictment. The Greenglasses testified that Julius Rosenberg had recruited them into a Soviet spy ring. Several weeks after their arrest, Congress passed the Internal Security Act of 1950, making it a crime to be a member of the Communist party.

Greenglass pled guilty to espionage and was given a fifteen-year prison sentence. His wife was never indicted. The Rosenbergs maintained their innocence, invoked the Fifth Amendment when asked if they were Communists, and were sentenced to death.

The extremely severe sentence brought about widespread support for clemency. Many were shocked because the Rosenbergs were the parents of two young sons, aged six and ten. There was a worldwide appeal to President Eisenhower from priests, educators, lawyers, writers, heads of states, even the Vatican. Yet Eisenhower remained unmoved.

In June 1953 the Rosenbergs made this statement through their attorney: "If we are executed, it will be murder of innocent people and the shame will be on the government of the United States. History will record, whether we live or not, that we were the victims of the most monstrous frame-up in the history of our country."

On the night of the execution, June 19, 1953, at 7:20 P.M., husband and wife said good-bye through a mesh screen, over which their fingertips touched in a final embrace.

Here is Julius Rosenberg's final letter to his friend and attorney, Manny Bloch, as well as the couple's final good-bye to their young children.

June 18, 1953

Dear Manny,

I have drawn up a last will and testament so that there can be no question about the fact that I want you to handle all our affairs and be responsible for the children as in fact you have been doing. Ethel completely concurs in this request and is in her own hand attesting to it.

Our children are the apple of our eye, our pride and most precious fortune. Love them with all your heart and always protect them in order that they grow up to be normal healthy people. That you will do this I am sure but as their proud father I take the prerogative to ask it of you my dearest friend and devoted brother. I love my sons most profoundly.

I am not much at saying good-byes because I believe that good accomplishments live on forever but this I can say my love of life has never been so strong because I've seen how beautiful the future can be. Since I feel that we in some small measure have contributed our share in this direction, I think my sons and millions of other[s] will have benefited by it.

Words fail me when I attempt to tell of the nobility and grandeur of my life's companion, my sweet and devoted wife. Ours is a great love, a wonderful relationship; it has made my life full and rich. . . .

You, Manny, are not only considered as one of my family but are our extra special friend. The bond of brotherhood and love between us was forged in the struggle for life and all that it means, and it is a source of great strength to us. Be strong for us beloved friend and we wish you long life to continue your fruitful work in health and happiness, for without doubt you are a fine man, dear friend, and sincere advocate of the people. I salute you and caress you affectionately with all my heart.

Never let them change the truth of our innocence.

For peace, bread, and roses in simple dignity we face the executioner with courage, confidence and perspective—never losing faith. . . .

As ever, Julie

JULIUS AND ETHEL ROSENBERG
to Their Children

June 19, 1953

Dearest Sweethearts, my most precious children,

Only this morning it looked like we might be together again after all. Now that this cannot be I want so much for you to know all that I have come to know. Unfortunately I may write only a few simple words; the rest your lives must teach you, even as mine taught me.

At first, of course, you will grieve bitterly for us, but you will not grieve alone. That is our consolation and it must eventually be yours. Eventually, too, you must come to believe that life is worth the living. Be comforted that even now, with the end of ours slowly approaching that we know this with a conviction that defeats the executioner!

Your lives must teach you, too, that good cannot really flourish in the midst of evil; that freedom and all the things that go to make up a truly satisfying and worthwhile life must sometimes be purchased very dearly. Be comforted, then, that we were serene and understood with the deepest kind of understanding that civilization had not as yet progressed to the point where life did not have to be lost for the sake of life; and that we were comforted in the sure knowledge that others would carry on after us.

We wish we might have had the tremendous joy and gratification of living our lives out with you. Your Daddy who is with me in these last momentous hours sends his heart and all the love that is in it for his dearest boys. Always remember that we were innocent and could not wrong our conscience.

We press you close and kiss you with all our strength.

Lovingly,
Daddy and Mommy—Julie Ethel

GEORGE BERNARD SHAW
to Stella Campbell

George Bernard Shaw's (1856–1950) career was marked by versatility and abundance. He wrote novels, drama and music reviews, and authored over fifty plays. Shaw's personal life was a complicated one. A married man, he nonetheless had a forty-year-long correspondence with Stella Campbell, a talented and radiant actress, with whom he had an intense and passionate relationship. Although there was always a question as to whether it was sexually consummated, it was by all accounts an intimate and long-standing involvement. Mrs. Campbell's husband, Patrick, had died in 1900, a year after she met Shaw. As a drama critic for the London **Saturday Review** *Shaw attended many of Campbell's performances. He wrote, "The moment she was seen, our reason collapsed and our judgement fled. . . . If the play was not tragic, our infatuation was." In 1912 he wrote the part of Eliza Doolittle, in his play* **Pygmalion**, *expressly for Campbell.*

Here Shaw expresses to Campbell his shock, anger, and grief upon hearing of the death of her only son, Alan, an acting lieutenant commander during World War I. On December 30, 1917, Alan and his commanding officer were standing at the top of the stairs of their dugout in La Vacquerie when a shell burst, killing both of them.

Jan. 7. 1918

Never saw it or heard about it until your letter came. It's no use: I can't be sympathetic; these things simply make me furious. I want to swear. I do swear. Killed just because people are blasted fools. A chaplain, too, to say nice things about it. It is not his business to say nice things about it, but to shout that the "voice of thy son's blood crieth unto God from the ground."

No, don't show me the letter. But I should very much like to have a nice talk with that dear Chaplain, that sweet sky-pilot, that . . .

No use going on like this, Stella. Wait for a week, and then I shall be very clever and broadminded again and have forgotten all about this. I shall be quite as nice as the Chaplain.

Oh, damn, damn, damn, damn, damn, damn, damn, damn, DAMN. And oh, dear, dear, dear, dear, dear, dearest!

G.B.S.

ABRAHAM LINCOLN
to Fanny McCullough

Abraham Lincoln (1809–1865) wrote this letter of condolence to Fanny McCullough, the daughter of his longtime friend, William McCullough. During Lincoln's law-circuit days, McCullough was sheriff and clerk of the McLean County Circuit Court in Bloomington, Illinois. Early in the Civil War he helped organize the Fourth Illinois Cavalry, where he served as lieutenant colonel. On December 5, 1862, he was killed during a night charge on a reconnaissance mission near Coffeeville, Mississippi. McCullough, who was overage and in poor health, was initially rejected when he tried to enlist, but so strong was his wish to fight on behalf of the Republic that he asked Lincoln to intercede on his behalf. Lincoln did so, and when McCullough was killed his death weighed heavily on Lincoln's mind. This letter shows the introspective and melancholy Lincoln. He speaks as a fellow mourner: the loss of his mother and that of his son Edward, who died at the age of four, shadowed him throughout his life.

December 23, 1862
Executive Mansion,
Washington, December 23, 1862

Dear Fanny,

It is with deep grief that I learn of the death of your kind and brave Father; and, especially, that it is affecting your young heart beyond what is common in such cases. In this sad world of ours, sorrow comes to all; and, to the young, it comes with bitterest agony, because it takes them unawares. The older have learned to ever expect it. I am anxious to afford some alleviation of your present distress. Perfect relief is not possible, except with time. You can not now realize that you will ever feel better. Is not this so? And yet it is a mistake. You are sure to be happy again. To know this, which is certainly true, will make you some less miserable now. I have had experience enough to know what I say; and you need only to believe it, to feel better at once. The memory of your dear Father, instead of an agony, will yet be a sad sweet feeling in your heart, of a purer and holier sort than you have known before.

Please present my kind regards to your afflicted mother.

Your sincere friend,
A. Lincoln

ABRAHAM LINCOLN
to Lydia Bixby

In the fall of 1864, Massachusetts Governor John A. Andrew wrote to President Lincoln asking him to express condolences to Mrs. Lydia Bixby, a widow who was believed to have lost five sons in the Civil War. Lincoln's letter to her was printed by the **Boston Evening Transcript** *and reprinted widely thereafter. However, later it was revealed that only two of Mrs. Bixby's five sons had actually died in battle. One deserted the army, one was honorably discharged, and another deserted or died a prisoner of war.*

Executive Mansion,
Washington, Nov. 21, 1864

Dear Madam,

I have been shown in the files of the War Department a statement of the Adjutant-General of Massachusetts that you are the mother of five sons who have died gloriously on the field of battle.

I feel how weak and fruitless must be any word of mine which should attempt to beguile you from the grief of a loss so overwhelming. But I cannot refrain from tendering you the consolation that may be found in the thanks of the Republic they died to save.

I pray that our Heavenly Father may assuage the anguish of your bereavement, and leave you only the cherished memory of the loved and lost, and the solemn pride that must be yours to have laid so costly a sacrifice upon the altar of freedom.

Yours, very sincerely and respectfully,
A. Lincoln

JOHN DONNE
to His Mother

John Donne (1572–1631) was regarded as the greatest of the meta-physical poets. An Anglican chaplain, he was known for his mesmerizing sermons, many of which highlighted his obsession with death. It was Donne who wrote the famous words "Any man's death diminishes me, because I am involved in mankind; and therefore never send to know for whom the bell tolls; it tolls for thee." His "Hymn to Christ at the Author's Last Going into Germany" is full of the apprehension of death, and weeks before his own demise he preached his last sermon, "Death's Duel," which was widely thought of as his own funeral sermon. In it he says, "God (with whom are the issues of death) hath delivered me from the death of the womb, by bringing me into the world, and from the manifold deaths of the world, by laying me in the grave." This letter, written in 1616, consoles his mother on the death of his sister Anne. Donne was left the only surviving child out of six.

1616

My most dear Mother,

When I consider so much of your life as can fall within my memory and observations, I find it to have been a sea, under a continual tempest, where one wave hath ever overtaken another. Our most wise and blessed Saviour chooseth what way it pleaseth Him to conduct those which He loves to His haven and eternal rest. The way which He hath chosen for you is strait, stormy, obscure and full of sad apparitions of death and wants, and sundry discomforts; and it has pleased Him that one discomfort should still succeed and touch another, that He might leave you no leisure, by any pleasure or abundance to stay or step out of that way, or almost take breath in that way, by which He hath determined to bring you home, which is His glorious Kingdom. . . .

I hope therefore, my most dear Mother, that your experience of the calamities of this life, your continual acquaintance with the visitations of the Holy Ghost, which gives better inward comforts than the world can outer discomforts, your wisdom to distinguish the value of this world from the next, and your religious fear of offending our merciful God by repining at anything which He doeth will preserve you from any inordinate and dangerous sorrow for the loss of my most beloved sister. For my part, which I am only left now to do the office of a child, though the poorness of my fortune, and the greatness of my charge, hath not suffered me to express my duty towards you as became me; yet I protest to you before Almighty God and His Angels and Saints in Heaven, that I do, and ever shall, esteem myself to be as strongly bound to look to you and provide for your relief, as for my own poor wife and children.

For whatsoever I shall be able to do I acknowledge to be a debt to you from whom I had that education which must make my fortune. . . . In the meantime, good mother, take heed that no sorrow nor dejection in your heart interrupt or disappoint God's purpose in you; His purpose is to remove out of your heart all such of this world's happiness as might put Him out of possession of it. He will have you entirely. . . .

JONATHAN SWIFT
to Alexander Pope

Jonathan Swift (1667–1745), Alexander Pope, and John Gay enjoyed an intimate correspondence as members of the Scriblerus Club, a group of close friends and letter writers, joined by their commitment to satire. Many people thought that the relationship between Swift and Pope was quarrelsome, a misconception that was based largely on the fact that Swift was deaf and Pope's physical frailty made it impossible for him to speak loudly. In fact, their admiration for each other was great. Pope once wrote to Swift that "No man living loves you better."

Although Swift and Pope were both satirists, their correspondence is tender. Swift, who was often called Dean because he was the dean of St. Patrick's in Dublin, wrote this letter to Pope on the death of John Gay, who died at the age of forty-six of an inflammatory fever. Although Swift's pain and self-pity are palpable, he can't help but compare the loss of friends to the loss of money; an incongruous and somewhat tactless comparison. Pope was devastated by Gay's death. Several months after he received this letter he wrote, "I have felt more, I fancy, in the loss of Mr. Gay than I shall suffer in the thought of going away myself into a state that can feel none of this sort of losses."

Dublin, January, 1733

I received yours with a few lines from the Doctor, and the account of our losing Mr. Gay, upon which event I shall say nothing. I am only concerned that long living hath not hardened me. For even in this Kingdom and in a few days past, two persons of great merit, whom I loved very well, have died in the prime of their years, but a little above thirty. I would endeavour to comfort myself upon the loss of friends, as I do upon the loss of money, by turning to my account book, and seeing whether I have enough left for my support; but in the former case I find I have not, any more than in the other; and I know not any man

who is in a greater likelihood than myself to die poor and friend-
less. You are a much greater loser than me by his death, as being
a more intimate friend, and often his companion, which latter I
could never hope to be, except perhaps once more in my life for
a piece of a summer. . . .

LADY MARY WORTLEY MONTAGU
to Her Daughter

Lady Mary Wortley Montagu (1689–1762) wrote witty and scandalous verse and published anonymous essays on feminist and political issues. She wrote prolifically but it was her skill as a letter writer that so awed her admirers. Her letter to her daughter, Lady Bute, on the death of Frederick, Prince of Wales, of whose court Lady Bute and her husband were members, is a masterly expression of Lady Mary's philosophy on coping with loss.

April 1751

My dear Child,
   'Tis impossible to tell you to what degree I share with you in the misfortune that has happened. I do not doubt your own reason will suggest to you all the alleviations that can serve on so sad an occasion, and will not trouble you with the commonplace topics that are used, generally to no purpose, in letters of consolation. Disappointment ought to be less sensibly felt at my age than yours; yet I own I am so far affected by this that I have need of all my philosophy to support it. However, let me beg of you not to indulge in useless grief, to the prejudice of your health, which is so necessary to your family. Everything may turn out better than you expect. We see so darkly into futurity, we never know when we have real cause to rejoice or lament. The worst appearances have often happy consequences, as the best lead many times into the greatest misfortunes. Human prudence is very straitly bounded. What is most in our power, though little so, is the disposition of our own minds. Do not give way to melancholy; seek amusements; be willing to be diverted, and insensibly you will become so. Weak people only place a merit in affliction. A grateful remembrance, and whatever honour we can pay to their memory is all that is owing to the dead.

Tears and sorrow are no duties to them, and make us incapable of those we owe to the living. . . .

. . . My dear child, endeavour to raise your spirits, and believe this advice comes from the tenderness of your most affectionate mother,

M. Wortley

My compliments and sincere condolence to Lord Bute.

SAMUEL JOHNSON
to James Elphinston

Samuel Johnson (1709–1784) was so often thought of as one of the most important writers of his time that the second half of the eighteenth century is often referred to as the Age of Johnson. In appearance John-son was unbathed and disheveled, but he was extremely well liked by everyone who made his acquaintance. Most famous for his **Dictionary of the English Language***, he was also considered a brilliant conver-sationalist and a great poet. The author of the periodical essays* **The Rambler***,* **The Adventurer***, and* **The Idler***, Johnson also edited Shakespeare and wrote several biographies as well as political satires. Here he suggests to his friend and Scottish publisher, James Elphinston, concrete ways in which to cope with the loss of his mother, Rachel Honey-man Elphinston. In it Johnson refers to a Mrs. Strahan, who was Elphinston's sister, to whom he wrote an account of their mother's death and funeral.*

September 25, 1750

Dear Sir,

You have, as I find by every kind of evidence, lost an excel-lent Mother; and I hope you will not think me incapable of par-taking of your grief. I have a Mother, now eighty-two years of age, whom, therefore, I must soon lose, unless it please God that she should rather mourn for me. I read the letters in which you relate your Mother's death to Mrs. Strahan, and think I do myself honour when I tell you that I read them with tears; but tears are neither to you nor to me of any further use, when once the tribute of nature has been paid. The business of life sum-mons us away from useless grief, and calls us to the exercise of those virtues of which we are lamenting our deprivation.

The greatest benefit which one friend can confer upon another is to guard and excite and elevate his virtues. This your mother will still perform, if you diligently preserve the memory of her life, and of her death; a life so far as I can learn, useful, wise, and innocent, and a death resigned, peaceful, and holy. I cannot forbear to mention, that neither reason nor revelation denies you to hope that you may increase her happiness by obeying her precepts; and that she may, in her present state, look with pleasure upon every act of virtue to which her instruction or example have contributed.

Whether this be more than a pleasing dream, or a just opinion of separate spirits, is indeed of no great importance to us, when we consider ourselves as acting under the eye of God: yet, surely, there is something pleasing in the belief that our separation from those whom we love is merely corporeal; and it may be a great incitement to virtuous friendship, if it can be made probable that that union that has received divine approbation shall continue to eternity.

There is one expedient by which you may in some degree continue her presence. If you write down minutely what you remember of her from your earliest years, you will read it with great pleasure, and receive from it many hints of soothing recollection, when time shall remove her yet further from you, and your grief shall be matured to veneration. To this, however, painful for the present, I cannot but advise you as to a source of comfort and satisfaction in the time to come; for all comfort and all satisfaction is sincerely wished you by, Dear Sir, Your most obliged, most obedient and most humble servant,

Sam Johnson

JAMES MICHENER
to His Friends

James Michener (1907–1997) was aware of his approaching death, and on October 9, 1997, he wrote this letter of farewell. He died just seven days later.

Dear Friends,

It is with a real sadness that I send you what looks to be a final correspondence between us. The medicos have left little doubt that this present illness is terminal. I approach this sad news with regret, but not with any panic. I am surrounded by friends who support me in these final moments with the same high spirit they have displayed in the past. And if anyone can keep a man's spirits elated, Debbie and Susan and John and Amelia can certainly do that. I am thus constantly fortified by young people of good spirits, who keep mine high.

I reach the end of my life with almost daily phone calls with beloved friends. Their spirits keep me alert and their reminiscences keep me alive. A constant hum of phone calls keeps me in touch with friends, who bring me joy and a sense of continuing life.

I wish I could visit each of you, but that would be impossible. The phone calls, however, recall the highlights of an exciting life. And they cascade back now to remind me of the highlights: the running for political office, and the drubbings we took there; the victories we had in the theatres. I savor every memory, as they parade past. What a full life they made. And what a joy they bring me now; what a joy your recollection of them gives me now. It is in this mood that my final days are being passed. And I thank you all for your thoughtfulness.

Fondly,
James A. Michener

WILLIAM COWPER
to John Newton

William Cowper (1731–1800) was a poet, a composer of hymns, a translator, and one of the great English letter writers. He was known not only for his poetic and literary talents but also for his intermittent bouts of insanity. He battled with depression, attempted suicide, and for periods of time was quite mad, or as he himself expressed it, "in total darkness." Reverend John Newton, the rector of St. Mary Woolnoth in London, also wrote verse and befriended Cowper after his second breakdown. It was Newton who encouraged Cowper to compose hymns (together they wrote over three hundred) and to undertake translations. For many years Cowper refused to have anything published without first sending it to Newton for guidance and editing. Cowper's religious themes and his belief that through poetry readers could find their way to God developed from early conversations with Newton.

When Newton's niece, Eliza Cunningham, whom he had adopted as his own daughter, died, Cowper wrote this letter of sympathy to his friend. It is an interesting addition to this collection in that the consoler actually congratulates the mourner.

October 16, 1785

My Dear Friend,—To have sent a child to Heaven is a great honour and a great blessing, and your feelings on such an occasion may well be such as render you rather an object of congratulation than of condolence. And were it otherwise, yet, having yourself free access to all the sources of genuine consolation, I feel that it would be little better than impertinence in me to suggest any. An escape from a life of suffering to a life of happiness and glory is such a deliverance as leaves no room for the sorrow of survivors, unless they sorrow for themselves. We cannot, indeed, lose what we love without regretting it; but a Christian is in possession of such alleviations of that regret, as the world knows nothing of. Their beloveds, when they die, go they know not whither; and if they suppose them, as they generally do, in a state of happiness, they have yet but an indifferent prospect of joining them in that state hereafter. But it is not so with you. You both know whither your beloved has gone, and you know that you shall follow her; and you know also that in the meantime she is incomparably happier than yourself. . . .

I have nothing to add, but that we are well, and remember you with much affection; and that I am, my dear friend,

Sincerely yours,
W.C.

SERVIUS SULPICIUS RUFUS
to Marcus Tullius Cicero

*Marcus Tullius Cicero was an orator, a statesman, and a man of let-
ters. A defender of the Republican cause, he was unsure whether to support Pompey and the aristocracy or Caesar and the new democracy. He
chose Pompey. Still Caesar allowed him to live peacefully in retirement.
When Caesar died, Cicero attempted to restore the Republic by working
against those who were soon to be in power, Octavian, Caesar's grand-
nephew, and Mark Antony. When he failed, Antony (who was particularly offended by a series of speeches Cicero delivered against him) had
Cicero murdered, cutting his hands off and his tongue out and nailing
them to a board for public viewing.*

    *Some two years before his own death, in 45 B.C., Cicero's twenty-
one-year-old daughter, Tullia, died in childbirth. Upon hearing of her
death, Servius Sulpicius Rufus (105–43 B.C.), the famous jurist, sent
Cicero this letter of condolence.*

March 45 B.C.

When I received the news of your daughter Tullia's death, I was
indeed as much grieved and distressed as I was bound to be, and
looked upon it as a calamity in which I shared. For, if I had been
at home, I should not have failed to be at your side, and should
have made my sorrow plain to you face to face. That kind of
consolation involves much distress and pain, because the relations and friends, whose part it is to offer it, are themselves overcome by an equal sorrow. They cannot attempt it without many
tears, so that they seem to require consolation themselves rather
than to be able to afford it to others. Still I have decided to set
down briefly for your benefit such thoughts as have occurred to
my mind, not because I suppose them to be unknown to you,
but because your sorrow may perhaps hinder you from being so
keenly alive to them. . . .

... Do not forget that you are Cicero, and a man accustomed to instruct and advise others; and do not imitate bad physicians, who in the diseases of others profess to understand the art of healing, but are unable to prescribe for themselves. Rather suggest to yourself and bring home to your own mind the very maxims which you are accustomed to impress upon others. There is no sorrow beyond the power of time at length to diminish and soften: it is a reflection on you that you should wait for this period, and not rather anticipate that result by the aid of your wisdom. But if there is any consciousness still existing in the world below, such was her love for you and her dutiful affection for all family, that she certainly does not wish you to act as you are acting. Grant this to her—your lost one! Grant it to your friends and comrades who mourn with you in your sorrow! ...

... I am ashamed to say any more to you on this subject, lest I should appear to distrust your wisdom. Therefore I will only make one suggestion before bringing my letter to an end. We have seen you on many occasions bear good fortune with a noble dignity which greatly enhanced your fame: now it is time for you to convince us that you are able to bear bad fortune equally well, and that it does not appear to you to be a heavier burden than you ought to think it. I would not have this be the only one of your virtues that you do not possess. ...

Good-bye.

CHARLOTTE BRONTË
to Ellen Nussey

*The novelist Charlotte Brontë (1816–1855) wrote this note to her friend Ellen Nussey after hearing of the death of Anne Carter, who had been a student of Charlotte's at the Roe Head School. Ellen and Charlotte loved each other dearly and corresponded with great regularity throughout their lives. It was Ellen's brother, Henry, who offered Charlotte her first proposal of marriage, which she turned down. This letter is an omen of the devastation and loss Brontë herself would feel as those closest to her died one by one. Her brother Branwell would die in September 1848, her sister Emily, author of **Wuthering Heights**, in December of that same year, and her remaining sister, Anne, in 1849. None of them lived past the age of thirty-one.*

January 12, 1840

Your letter, which I received this morning, was one of painful interest. Anne Carter it seems, is dead; when I saw her last she was a young, beautiful and happy girl; now "life's fitful fever" is over with her and she "sleeps well." I shall never see her again. It is a sorrowful thought for she was a warm-hearted, affectionate being, and I cared for her. Wherever I seek her now in this world she cannot be found, no more than a flower or a leaf which withered twenty years ago. A bereavement of this kind gives one a glimpse of the feeling those must have who have seen all drop round them, friend after friend, and are left to end their pilgrimage alone. But tears are fruitless, and I try not to repine.

CHARLOTTE BRONTË
to Ellen Nussey

After Emily had died and Anne's death was fast approaching, Charlotte wrote again to Ellen Nussey.

December 23, 1848

My dear Ellen,

Emily suffers no more from pain or weakness now. She never will suffer more in this world. She is gone, after a hard, short conflict. She died on Tuesday, the very day I wrote to you. I thought it very possible she might be with us still for weeks; and a few hours afterwards, she was in eternity. Yes, there is no Emily in time or on earth now. Yesterday we put her poor, wasted, mortal frame quietly under the church pavement. We are very calm at present. Why should we be otherwise? The anguish of seeing her suffer is over; the spectacle of the pains of death is gone by; the funeral day is past. We feel she is at peace. No need now to tremble for the hard frost and the keen wind. Emily does not feel them. She died in a time of promise. We saw her taken from life in its prime. But it is God's will, and the place where she is gone is better than she has left.

God has sustained me, in a way that I marvel at, through such agony as I had not conceived. I now look to Anne, and wish she were well and strong; but she is neither; nor is papa. Could you now come to us for a few days? I would not ask you to stay long. Write and tell me if you could come next week, and by what train. . . . You will, I trust, find us tranquil. Try to come. I never so much needed the consolation of a friend's presence. Pleasure, of course, there would be none for you in the visit, except what your kind heart would teach you to find in doing good to others.

Several weeks after Anne died, Charlotte wrote, "My life is what I expected it to be. . . . I wake and know that Solitude, Remembrance, and Longing are to be almost my sole companions. . . . To sit in a lonely room—the clock ticking loud through a still house—and have open before the mind's eye the record of the last year, with its shocks, sufferings and losses—is a trial."

SIR WILLIAM OSLER
to His Wife

Sir William Osler (1849–1919), professor of medicine, was one of the most beloved physicians in the English-speaking world. He transformed medical education in the United States by stressing the privileges of being a physician and teaching students to treat the patient as well as the disease. As a warm-hearted and available mentor, he also altered the traditionally cold and formal professor–student relationship. Osler and his wife were thrilled when she gave birth to their son, Paul Revere Osler. But within a week, the child was dead. In a sweet and tender attempt to console his wife, and perhaps himself, Osler wrote a letter in the guise of his dead son. Postmarked "Heaven," it tells his mother of his heavenly existence.

February 1893

Dear Mother,

If we are good & get on nicely with our singing & if our earthly parents continue to show an interest in us by remembering us in their prayers, we are allowed to write every three or four tatmas (i.e., month). I got here safely with very little inconvenience. I scarcely knew anything until I awoke in a lovely green spot, with fountains & trees & soft couches & such nice young girls to tend us. You would have been amused to see the hundreds which came the same day.

But I must tell you first how we are all arranged; it took me several days to find out about it. Heaven is the exact counterpart of earth so far as its dwellers are concerned, thus all from the US go to one place—all from Maryland to one district & even all from the cities & townships get corresponding places. This enables the guardian angels to keep the lists more carefully & it facilitates communication between relatives. They are most particular in this respect & have a beautifully simple arrangement by which the new arrivals can find out at once whether they have connections in Heaven. I never was more surprised in my time—we say that here, not life & not eternity for that has not started for us—when the day after my arrival Althea brought me two quill feathers on one of which was written Julius Caesar & the other Emma Osler. I knew at once about the former . . . but the latter I did not know at all, but she said she had been father's little sister & she had been sent to make me feel happy & comfortable. . . .

Unlike the real angels we have no foreknowledge & cannot tell what is to happen to our dear ones on earth. Next to the great feast days, when we sing choruses by divisions in the upper heavens, our chief delight is in watching the soul bodies as they arrive in our divisions & in helping the angels to get them in order and properly trained. In the children's divisions not a friad (i.e., about an hour of earthly time) passes without the excitement of a father or mother, a brother or a sister united to one of us. We know about 1000 of each other so that it is great fun to see our comrades & friends making their relatives feel at home. . . .

GEORGE GORDON, LORD BYRON
to John Cam Hobhouse

Within a very short period of time the English poet George Gordon, Lord Byron (1788–1824), lost his mother, whom he adored, and then in quick succession two of his most loved and valued friends, John Wingfield and Charles Skinner Matthews. Here Byron grieves in a letter to his old friend John Cam Hobhouse on the loss of Matthews, who had drowned. Hobhouse and Byron, along with Scrope Berdmore Davies, were contemporaries at Cambridge and they all remained close friends. Byron's letters to Hobhouse are among his most candid and revealing. Byron cared deeply for Hobhouse and in an earlier letter to their mutual friend Davies, Byron wrote, "What will our poor Hobhouse feel! His letters breathe but of Matthews."

Newstead Abbey, August 10, 1811

My dear Hobhouse—From Davies I had already received the death of Matthews, & from M[atthews] a letter dated the day before his death. In that letter he mentions you, & as it was perhaps the last he ever wrote, you will derive a poor consolation from hearing that he spoke of you with that affectionate familiarity, so much more pleasing from those we love than the highest encomiums of the World.

My dwelling, you already know, is the House of Mourning, & I am really so much bewildered with the different shocks I have sustained that I can hardly reduce myself to reason by the most frivolous occupations. My poor friend, J. Wingfield, my Mother, & your best friend, & (surely not the worst of mine) C[harles] S[kinner] M[atthews] have disappeared in one little month since my return, & without my seeing either, though I have heard from All.

There is to me something so incomprehensible in death, that I can neither speak or think on the subject. Indeed when I looked on the Mass of Corruption, which was the being from whence I sprang, I doubted within myself whether I was, or She was not. I have lost her who gave me being, & some of those who made that Being a blessing. I have neither hopes nor fears beyond the Grave, yet if there is within us a "spark of that Celestial Fire" M has already "mingled with the Gods."

In the room where I now write (flanked by the Skulls you have seen so often) did you & M & myself pass some joyous unprofitable evenings, & here we will drink to his Memory, which though it cannot reach the dead, will soothe the Survivors, & to them only death can be an Evil—I can neither receive or administer Consolation. Time will do it for us. In the Interim let me see or hear from you, if possible both. I am very lonely, & should think myself miserable, were it not for a kind of hysterical merriment, which I can neither account for, or conquer, but, strange as it is, I do laugh & heartily, wondering at myself while I sustain it. I have tried reading, & boxing, & swimming, & writing, & rising early, & sitting late, & water, & wine, with a number of ineffectual remedies, & here I am, wretched, but not "melancholy or gentlemanlike." My dear 'Cam of the Cornish' (M's last expression!!) may Man or God give you the happiness, which I wish rather than expect you may attain; believe me none living are more sincerely yours than Byron.

JOHANN WOLFGANG VON GOETHE
to His Grandmother

Johann Wolfgang von Goethe (1749–1832) was a dramatist, statesman, scientist, lawyer, and philosopher. He served as prime minister of the state of Weimar, was the author of **Faust***, and is considered to be the single greatest German lyric poet. Not many know that he also put forth the theory of a common origin for all life forms, paving the way for Darwinism. The letter that follows was written to his maternal grandmother on the death at the age of seventy-eight of his grandfather, Johann Wolfgang Textor, who was chief magistrate and imperial counselor of Frankfurt.*

February 1771

Dearest Grandmama,

The death of our dear father, already dreaded from day to day for so long a time, has yet come upon me unprepared. I have felt this loss with all my heart; and what to us is the world around us, when we lose what we love?

To console myself, and not you, I write to you, you who are now the head of our family to beg you for your love, and assure you of my tenderest devotion. You have lived longer in the world than I, and must find in your own heart more comfort than I know of. You have endured more misfortune than I; you must feel far more vividly than I can say it that the most sorrowful occurrence often, through the hand of Providence, takes the most favorable turn for our happiness; that the succession of fortune and misfortune in life is intertwined like sleep and waking, neither without the other, and one for the sake of the other; that all happiness in the world is only lent.

You have seen children and grandchildren die before you, ceasing their work in the morning of their life; and now your tears accompany a husband to the everlasting Sabbath rest—a man who has honestly earned his wage. He has it now; and yet the good God, whilst he took thought for him has also taken thought for you—for us. He has taken from us not the merry friendly, happy old man who carried on the affairs of the age with the vivacity of a youth, who stood out amongst his fellow-citizens and was the joy of his family. He has now taken from us a man whose life we have seen for some years hanging by a silken thread. His energetic spirit must have felt with painful heaviness the oppressive weight of his sickly body; must have wished himself free, as a prisoner yearns to escape from his cell.

Now he is free, and our tears bid him God-speed; and our sorrow gathers us around you, dear Mama, to console ourselves with you, hearts simply full of love. You have lost much, but much remains to you. Look at us, love us, and be happy. May you enjoy for a long time yet the temporal reward which you have so richly earned of our invalid father, who has gone hence to report it at the place of requital and who has left us behind as tokens of his love, tokens of the past time of sorrowful yet pleasing recollection.

And so may your love for us remain as it was; and where much love is, there is much happiness.

I am, with a truly warm heart, your loving grandchild,

J. W. Goethe

SAMUEL TAYLOR COLERIDGE
to Charles Lamb

Samuel Taylor Coleridge (1772–1834), the poet, dramatist, political journalist, essayist, and lecturer, and Charles Lamb, the critic, author, and poet, were lifelong friends. They met as children at Christ's Hospital School, a charity boarding school in London. Lamb was devoted to Coleridge, who introduced him to the world of literature and opened his mind to fresh ideas, and looked up to him as to an older brother. But the relationship was hardly one-sided, for Lamb became Coleridge's advisor on practical and personal matters. They confided in each other and were devoted to each other all of their lives.

When Lamb was twenty-one he endured a devastating episode. At home with his sister, Mary, and their infirm parents, he watched as his sister seized a knife and plunged it into their mother's heart. It was said that Mary was driven insane by her disabled parents' total dependency on her. Indeed, the jury's verdict was lunacy and she was committed to an asylum. Lamb was naturally very shaken and wrote to Coleridge with an account of his mother's death. He ended the letter by asking Coleridge to respond with "as religious a letter as possible." This letter is Coleridge's reply.

September 28, 1796

Your letter, my friend, struck me with a mighty horror. It rushed upon me and stupefied my feelings. You bid me write you a religious letter; I am not a man who would attempt to insult the greatness of your anguish by any other consolation. Heaven knows that in the easiest fortunes there is much dissatisfaction and weariness of spirit; much that calls for the exercise of patience and resignation; but in storms, like these, that shake the dwelling and make the heart tremble, there is no middle way between despair and the yielding up of the whole spirit unto the guidance of faith. And surely it is a matter of joy, that your faith in Jesus has been preserved; the Comforter that should relieve you is not far from you. But as you are a Christian, in the name of that Saviour, who was filled with bitterness and made drunken with wormwood, I conjure you to have recourse in frequent prayer to "his God and your God"; the God of mercies, and father of all comfort.

Your poor father is, I hope, almost senseless of the calamity; the unconscious instrument of Divine Providence knows it not, and your mother is in heaven. It is sweet to be roused from a frightful dream by the song of birds and the gladsome rays of the morning. Ah, how infinitely more sweet to be awakened from the blackness and amazement of a sudden horror by the glories of God manifest and the hallelujahs of angels.

As to what regards yourself, I approved altogether of your abandoning what you justly call vanities. I look upon you as a man, called by sorrow and anguish and a strange desolation of hopes into quietness, and a soul set apart and made peculiar to God! We cannot arrive at any portion of heavenly bliss without in some measure imitating Christ. And they arrive at the largest inheritance who imitate the most difficult parts of his character, and bowed down and crushed under foot cry in fullness of faith, "Father, thy will be done."

I wish above measure to have you for a little while here; no visitants shall blow on the nakedness of your feelings; you shall be quiet, and your spirit may be healed. I see no possible objection, unless your father's helplessness prevent you, and unless you are necessary to him. If this be not the case, I charge you write me that you will come.

I charge you, my dearest friend, not to dare to encourage gloom or despair. You are a temporary sharer in human miseries, that you may be an eternal partaker of the Divine nature. I charge you, if by any means it be possible, come to me.

I remain, your affectionate,

S. T. Coleridge

RALPH WALDO EMERSON
to Mary Moody Emerson

Ralph Waldo Emerson (1803–1882), the popular American philosopher, poet, lecturer, and essayist, had grieved much in his life. His father had died a few weeks before Emerson's eighth birthday. In 1831 his bride of less than two years, Ellen, succumbed to tuberculosis. In 1834 and 1836 he was mourning the loss of his brothers, Edward and Charles. But in 1842 he suffered his most agonizing blow when his five-year-old son, Waldo, died of scarlatina (scarlet fever). Emerson wrote to his aunt, Mary Moody Emerson, of his grief. Mary was the single most important influence on Emerson during his formative years. She, too, was a writer and Emerson edited much of her work.

Concord
January 28, 1842

My dear Aunt,

My boy, my boy is gone. He was taken ill of Scarlatina on Monday evening, and died last night. I can say nothing to you. My darling and the world's wonderful child, for never in my own or another family have I seen any thing comparable, has fled out of my arms like a dream. He adorned the world for me like a morning star, and every particular of my daily life. I slept in his neighborhood and woke to remember him. . . .

. . . I can only tell you now that my angel has vanished. You too will grieve for the little traveller, though you scarce have seen his features.

Farewell, dear Aunt.
Waldo E.

RALPH WALDO EMERSON
to Thomas Carlyle

When Emerson learned of the death of Thomas Carlyle's wife, Jane, he immediately wrote this sincere and touching letter to his friend. The Scot Carlyle and the American Emerson were writers of equal rank but they could not have been more different in principle and temperament, Carlyle being essentially an empiricist and Emerson an idealist. Yet they maintained a lifelong friendship, with Emerson acting as Carlyle's American agent.

Although Jane Carlyle had long been in poor health, suffering from headaches, sleeplessness, and the excruciating pain of neuralgia in her hands, she was an outgoing and well-educated woman and often helped Carlyle with his writing. At the time of her death, Carlyle was at Edinburgh University, where he had delivered the university's inaugural address, a copy of which he had sent to his wife, who had the chance to read it two days before she died.

Concord
May 16, 1866

My dear Carlyle,

I have just been shown a private letter from Moncure Conway to one of his friends here, giving some tidings of your sad return to an empty home. We had the first news last week. And so it is. The stroke long threatened has fallen at last, in the mildest form to its victim, & relieved to you by long & repeated reprieves. I must think her fortunate also in this gentle departure, as she had been in her serene & honoured career. We would not for ourselves count covetously the descending steps, after we have passed the top of the mount, or grudge to spare some of the days of decay. And you will have the peace of knowing her safe & no longer a victim. I have found myself recalling an old verse which one utters to the parting soul:

For thou has passed all change of human life,
And not again to thee shall beauty die.

It is thirty years, I think, since I last saw her, & her conversation & faultless manners gave assurance of a good & happy future. As I have not witnessed any decline, I can hardly believe in any, & still recall vividly the youthful wife & her blithe account of her letters & homages from Goethe, & the details she gave of her intended visit to Weimar, & its disappointment. Her goodness to me & to my friends was ever perfect & all Americans have agreed in her praise. Elizabeth Hoar remembers her with entire sympathy & regard.

I could heartily wish to see you for an hour in these lonely days. Your friends, I know, will approach you as tenderly as friends can; & I can believe that labor—all whose precious secrets you know—will prove a consoler—though it cannot quite avail—for she was the rest that rewarded labor. It is good that you are strong, & built for endurance. Nor will you shun to consult the aweful oracles which in these hours of tenderness are sometimes vouchsafed. If to any, to you.

I rejoice that she stayed to enjoy the knowledge of your good day at Edinburgh, which is a leaf we would not spare from your book of life. It was a right manly speech to be so made, & is a voucher of unbroken strength—& the surroundings, as I learn, were all the happiest—with no hint of change. I pray you bear in mind your own counsels. Long years you must still achieve, & I hope neither grief nor weariness will let you "join the dim choir of the bards that have been," until you have written the book I wish & wait for—the sincerest confessions of your best hours. My wife prays to be remembered to you with sympathy & affection.

Ever yours faithfully,
R. W. Emerson

HENRY WADSWORTH LONGFELLOW
to Mary Appleton Mackintosh

Henry Wadsworth Longfellow (1807–1882) lost his first wife in 1835, after only four years of marriage. His beloved second wife, Fanny, who became the mother of his six children, died in a terrible accident in July 1861. Fanny and the couple's two daughters were sitting in the library of their home sealing small packages of their curls with hot wax, when Fanny dropped a match, which swiftly ignited her cotton dress. The children were unharmed but Fanny died the next day. Her funeral was held three days later, but Longfellow, who suffered serious burns trying to save his wife by wrapping her body in a rug, was confined to his bed. He was devastated and wrote to a friend, "[I am] to the eyes of others outwardly calm; but inwardly bleeding to death." In August he wrote this heartbreaking letter to his sister-in-law, Mary Appleton Mackintosh, Fanny's sister. Longfellow's father-in-law, Nathan Appleton, had died on July 14, the day after Fanny's funeral.

Dearest Mary,

I will try to write you a line today, if only to thank you for your affectionate letter, which touched and consoled me much.

How I am alive after what my eyes have seen, I know not. I am at least patient, if not resigned; and thank God hourly—as I have from the beginning for the beautiful life we led together, and that I loved her more and more to the end.

Truly do you say there was no one like her. And now that she is gone, I can only utter a cry "from the depth of divine Despair." If I could be with you for a while, I should be greatly comforted, only to you can I speak out all that is in my heart about her. . . .

I am afraid I am very selfish in my sorrow; but not an hour passes without my thinking of you, and of how you will bear the double woe, of a father's and a sister's death at once. Dear affectionate old man! The last day of his life, all day long, he sat holding a lily in his hand, a flower from Fanny's funeral. I trust that the admirable fortitude and patience which thus far have supported you will not fail. Nor must you think that having preached resignation to others I am myself a castaway. Infinite tender memories of our darling fill me and surround me. Nothing but sweetness comes from her. That noble, loyal, spiritual nature always uplifted and illumined mine, and always will, to the end.

For the future I have no plans. I can not yet lift my eyes in that direction. I only look backward, not forward. The only question is, what will be the best for the children? I shall think of that when I get back to Cambridge.

Meanwhile think of me here by this haunted sea-shore. So strong is the sense of her presence upon me, that I should hardly be surprised to meet her in our favourite walk, or, if I looked up now, to see her in the room.

My heart aches and bleeds sorely for the poor children. To lose such a mother, and all the divine influences of her character and care. They do not know how great their loss is, but I do. God will provide. His will be done! Full of affection, ever most truly,

HWL

ROBERT FALCON SCOTT
to James Matthew Barrie

In 1902 British Navy Captain Robert Falcon Scott (1868–1912) organized the National Antarctic Expedition. For three years he traveled the ice-covered stretches of the Antarctic and acquired the experience and scientific data necessary for a second expedition, which would take him to the South Pole. But when Scott and his crew arrived at the Pole they were met by Norwegian mariner Roald Amundsen, who had preceded them by thirty-five days. Disappointed, they began the seven-hundred-mile journey home.

Gale-force blizzards, frostbite, and unbearable temperatures of forty degrees below zero were too much for the men to bear. Soon their supplies ran low and Scott knew that the end was not far. He began to write several letters of farewell to his friends and family and to the wives and children of several of his crew, who were unable to write themselves. In one he wrote, "Had we lived, I should have had a tale to tell of the hardihood, endurance, and courage of my companions which would have stirred the heart of every Englishman. These rough notes and our dead bodies must tell the tale. . . ." Here he writes to his friend, James Matthew Barrie, the novelist who is well-known as the creator of Peter Pan. It is a rare testament of friendship and an eloquent appeal for Barrie to watch over Scott's widow and child. Eight months after this letter was written the bodies of Scott and two of his crew were found just fifteen miles from the nearest supply camp.

March 1912

We are pegging out in a very comfortless spot. Hoping this letter may be found and sent to you, I write a word of farewell. . . . More practically, I want you to help my widow and my boy— your godson.

Good-bye, I am not at all afraid of the end, but sad to miss many a humble pleasure which I had planned for the future on our long marches. I may not have proved a great explorer, but we have done the greatest march ever made and come very near to great success. Good-bye, my dear friend.

We are in a desperate state, feet frozen, no fuel and a long way from food; but it would do your heart good to be in our tent, to hear our songs and the cheery conversation as to what we will do when we get to Hunt Point.

Later. We are very near the end, but have not and will not lose our good cheer. We have had four days of storm in our tent, and nowhere food or fuel. We did intend to finish ourselves when things proved like this, but we have decided to die naturally in the track.

As a dying man, my dear friend, be good to my wife and child. Give the boy a chance in life if the State won't do it. He ought to have good stuff in him.

I never met a man in my life whom I admired and loved more than you, and I never could show you how much your friendship meant to me, for you had much to give and I nothing.

HERMAN HESSE
to Thomas Mann

Novelists and Nobel Prize Laureates Herman Hesse (1877–1962) and Thomas Mann met in 1904 when they were considered the two most promising young German writers of the day. Together they were co-defenders of the humanistic tradition in German culture. But Hesse's romanticism was the polar opposite of Mann's realism, and they led radically different lives. Hesse was disappointed in his personal life and isolated himself almost to the point of seclusion, his contact with the public limited to his prodigious literary output. Mann married success-fully and had six children. He lectured widely and was an unofficial cultural spokesman for the Weimar Republic. Despite their differences the two men greatly admired each other and maintained one of the richest and longest-lasting literary friendships on record. Upon Hesse's sixtieth birthday Mann wrote, "I long ago chose him as the member of my literary generation closest and dearest to me."

It is estimated, conservatively, that Herman Hesse wrote more than 35,000 letters in his lifetime. When Hesse learned that Mann's son, Klaus, also an author, had committed suicide he wrote this sensitive let-ter to his friend. Hesse refers to "the shortcomings of his [Klaus's] liter-ary efforts." Hesse had taken issue with a discrepancy in Klaus's early work but was impressed with his last book, **André Gide and the Cri-sis of** *Modern Thought.*

May 26, 1949

Dear Herr Thomas Mann,

Like all your friends, we have received the sad news with consternation and profound sympathy. We old people are used to having our friends and traveling companions taken from us, but there is something terrifying about losing someone close to us belonging to the generation which, we thought, would take our places when we go and in a measure shield us from the eternal silence. That is hard to take.

I don't know much about how you stood to Klaus. I myself followed his beginnings with attentive sympathy. Later on I was sometimes troubled for your sake by the shortcomings of his literary efforts, but today I find consolation in the thought that these efforts finally culminated in a fine valuable work, which surpassed them—his book on André Gide. This book, which won the hearts of his friends and yours, will long survive its author.

In these days we are thinking more than ever of you and your wife. We press your hands in heartfelt sympathy.

Yours ever,
Hermann Hesse

HERMAN HESSE
to Thomas Mann

Scarcely a year later, Mann lost his brother, Heinrich. Once again, Hesse was there to offer sympathy to his old friend.

March 17, 1950

Dear Herr Thomas Mann,

With deep sympathy I have read the news of your brother's death. Of all the strange and ambivalent things that old age brings us, the loss of our intimates, especially the companions of our youth, is perhaps the strangest. As little by little they all vanish away, so that in the end we have more friends and intimates in the "beyond" than here below, we become curious about this beyond and lose the dread of it we had when they walked us around more securely.

But with all our losses and all the loosening of our roots, we don't put aside our egoism. And so, at the news of this death, after I had taken it in and accustomed myself to it, my second and strongest thought was of you, and the hope that this leave-taking may not make the thought of your own leave-taking too easy for you comes quite spontaneously and selfishly to my heart and lips.

Yes, I fervently hope that your light may long continue to shine. It gives me strength to know you are still there and accessible.

With warm regards from us both to you both.

Cordially,
H. Hesse

C. S. LEWIS
to Owen Barfield

Irish-born writer Clive Staples Lewis (1898–1963) was a literary historian, a Christian apologist, and the author of science fiction and children's stories as well as works on literature and religion. Over the years he gained a scholarly reputation as a lecturer on medieval and Renaissance English literature, a subject he taught at Cambridge University. In 1936 Lewis wrote to author Charles Williams, who had recently completed **The Place of the Lion.** *Lewis praised the novel and suggested they meet. Strangely enough, Williams had just written Lewis praising his* **Allegorical Love Poem.** *Williams wrote, "If you had delayed writing another 24 hours our letters would have crossed. It has never before happened to me to be admiring an author of a book while he at the same time was admiring mine." Lewis cherished Williams' friendship immensely and was shocked by the untimely death of his friend, "the most angelic man." Lewis rushed to see Williams, who had been seized with pain and taken to the hospital. But he was too late. Here Lewis muses freely on Williams' death in a letter to their mutual friend, Owen Barfield.*

May 18, 1945

It has been a very odd experience. This, the first really severe loss I have suffered has: (a) given a corroboration to my belief in immortality such as I never dreamed of—it is almost tangible now; (b) swept away all my old feelings of mere horror and disgust at funerals, coffins, graves, etc.—if need had been I think I could have handled that corpse with hardly any unpleasant sensations; (c) greatly reduced my feeling about ghosts. I think (but who knows?) that I should be, though afraid, more pleased than afraid if his turned up. . . . To put it in a nutshell, what the idea of death has done to him is nothing to what he has done to the idea of death. . . .

CHARLES DICKENS
to John Forster

Author Charles Dickens (1812–1870) wrote this letter to his dear friend John Forster after he heard of the death of Forster's only brother, Christopher. Forster was a barrister but devoted most of his life to writing as a journalist and literary critic. After Dickens' death it was Forster who wrote the much-admired **Life of Charles Dickens**, *which included this moving letter. Forster wrote, "Dickens had a friend's true helpfulness in sorrow. I permit myself to preserve in a note for what it relates of his own sad experiences and solemn beliefs and hopes."*

January 8, 1845

I feel the distance between us now, indeed. I would to Heaven, my dearest friend, that I could remind you in a manner more lively and affectionate than this dull sheet of paper can put on, that you have a Brother left. One bound to you by ties as strong as ever Nature forged. By ties never to be broken, weakened, changed in any way—but to be knotted tighter up, if that be possible, until the same end comes to them as has come to these. That end but the bright beginning of a happier union, I believe; and have never more strongly and religiously believed (and oh! Forster, with what a sore heart I have thanked God for it!) than when that shadow has fallen on my own hearth, and made it cold and dark. . . .

When you write to me again, the pain of this will have passed. No consolation can be so certain and so lasting to you as that softened and manly sorrow which springs up from the memory of the Dead. I read your heart as easily as if I held it in my hand, this moment. And I know—I know, my dear friend— that before the ground is green above him, you will be content that what was capable of death in him, should lie there. I am glad to think it was so easy, and full of peace. What can we hope for more, when our own time comes! The day when he visited us in our old house is as fresh to me as if it had been yesterday. I remember him as well as I remember you . . . I have many things to say, but cannot say them now.

Your attached and loving friend of life, and far, I hope, beyond it,

CD

CHARLES DICKENS
to His Wife

Several years later Forster accompanied Dickens to a meeting of the General Theatrical Fund where Dickens was to deliver a speech. Half an hour before the event, and for some unknown reason, Forster was called out of the room by a servant and notified of the sudden death of Dickens' infant daughter, Dora Annie. Forster thought it best to let him deliver his speech and then told him the terrible news. As Dickens' wife, Catherine, was vacationing outside of London, Forster was asked to deliver this letter to prepare her for the news of her child's death and to bring her home.

April 15, 1851

My dearest Kate,

Now observe, you must read this letter very slowly and carefully. If you have hurried on thus far without quite understanding (apprehending some bad news) I rely on your turning back and reading again.

Little Dora, without being in the least pain, is suddenly stricken ill. There is nothing in her appearance but perfect rest—you would suppose her quietly asleep, but I am sure she is very ill, and I cannot encourage myself with much hope of her recovery. I do not—why should I say I do to you, my dear!—I do not think her recovery at all likely.

I do not like to leave home. I can do no good here, but I think it right to stay here. You will not like to be away, I know, and I cannot reconcile it to myself to keep you away. Forster, with his usual affection for us, comes down to bring you this letter and to bring you home, but I cannot close it without putting the strongest entreaty and injunction upon you to come with perfect composure—to remember what I have often told you, that we never can expect to be exempt, as to our many children, from the afflictions of other parents, and that if—if when you come I should even have to say to you, "our little baby is dead," you are to do your duty to the rest, and to show yourself worthy of the great trust you hold in them.

If you will only read this steadily I have a perfect confidence in your doing what is right.—Ever affectionately.

ABIGAIL ADAMS
to Thomas Jefferson

Thomas Jefferson and Abigail Adams (1744–1818) did not end their lives in friendship. Regardless of the historic relationship between Jefferson and Abigail's husband, John Adams, Abigail was furious at Jefferson for dismissing her son, John Quincy Adams, from a lucrative government position. Nonetheless when Jefferson's daughter Mary Eppes died, Abigail was distraught. When Mary was a young girl she had been left in Abigail's care in England. Abigail writes beautifully and directly in this emotional letter of condolence to Jefferson. Jefferson later responded with an enormously affectionate letter, expressing hope that their relationship would resume, but the friendship was never fully restored.

May 20, 1804

Sir,

Had you been no other than the private inhabitant of Monticello, I should, ere this time, have addressed you with that sympathy which a recent event has awakened in my bosom; but reasons of various kinds withheld my pen, until the powerful feelings of my heart have burst through the restraint, and called upon me to shed the tear of sorrow over the departed remains of your beloved and deserving daughter. An event which I most sincerely mourn.

The attachment which I formed for her when you committed her to my care upon her arrival in a foreign land, under circumstances peculiarly interesting, has remained with me to this hour; and the recent account of her death, which I read in a late paper, recalled to my recollection the tender scene of her separation from me, when, with the strongest sensibility, when she clung around my neck and wet my bosom with her tears, saying,

"O! now I have learned to love you, why will they take me from you."

It has been some time since I conceived that any event in this life could call forth feelings of mutual sympathy. But I know how closely entwined around a parents heart are those cords which bind the parental to the filial bosom; and when snapped asunder, how agonizing the pangs. I have tasted the bitter cup, and bow with reverence and humility before the great Dispenser of it, without whose permission and overruling providence not a sparrow falls to the ground. That you may derive comfort and consolation in this day of your sorrow and affliction from that only source calculated to heal the broken heart, a firm belief in the being, perfections and attributes of God, is the sincere and ardent wish of her who once took pleasure in subscribing herself your friend.

Abigail Adams

THOMAS JEFFERSON
to John Adams

When Jefferson (1743–1826) learned that Abigail Adams had died from typhoid fever, he wrote this letter of condolence to his friend John Adams.

Monticello
November 13, 1818

The public papers, my dear friend, announce the fatal event of which your letter of Oct. 20 had given me ominous foreboding. Tried myself, in the school of affliction, by the loss of every form of connection which can rive the human heart, I know well, and feel what you have lost, what you have suffered, are suffering, and have yet to endure. The same trials have taught me that, for ills so immeasurable, time and silence are the only medicines. I will not therefore, by useless condolences, open afresh the sluices of your grief nor, although mingling sincerely my tears with yours, will I say a word more, where words are vain, but that it is of some comfort to us both that the term is not very distant at which we are to deposit, in the same cerement, our sorrows and suffering bodies, and to ascend in essence to an ecstatic meeting with the friends we have loved and lost and whom we shall still love and never lose again. God bless you and support you under your heavy affliction.

Th. Jefferson

VIRGINIA WOOLF
to Leonard Woolf

Writer Virginia Woolf (1882–1941) was one of the pioneers of modern fiction. She was a member, along with Lytton Strachey, E. M Forster, Clive Bell, and others, of the English artistic and literary Bloomsbury group. In addition to her novels, she became well-known as an essayist, as a popular lecturer on literature and women's rights, and for her strong stance against censorship. But her abilities were marred by manic-depressive illness and toward the end of her life she was plagued by voices in her head and constant mood swings. She was aware that her sanity was waning and loathed the burden she had become to her devoted husband, writer Leonard Woolf.

On March 28, 1941, she went into her studio and wrote farewell letters to the people she loved most, Leonard (to whom she wrote two with similar contents) and her sister, Vanessa, to whom she wrote, "I have fought against it, but I can't any longer." Her madness had become too much for her to bear. She placed the notes on the mantelpiece in her living room and made her way through the meadows. She put her walking stick and her hat on the bank of the River Ouse and placed a large stone in her coat pocket. She walked into the water and never emerged. Her body was found downstream on April 18. Here is one of her letters to Leonard.

March 28, 1941

Dearest,

I feel certain I am going mad again. I feel we can't go through another of those terrible times. And I shan't recover this time. I begin to hear voices, and I can't concentrate. So I am doing what seems the best thing to do. You have given me the greatest possible happiness. You have been in every way all that anyone could be. I don't think two people could have been happier till this terrible disease came. I can't fight any longer. I know that I am spoiling your life, that without me you could work. And you will I know. You see I can't even write this properly. I can't read. What I want to say is I owe all the happiness of my life to you. You have been entirely patient with me and incredibly good. I want to say that—everybody knows it. If anybody could have saved me it would have been you. Everything has gone from me but the certainty of your goodness. I can't go on spoiling your life any longer.

I don't think two people could have been happier than we have been.

V.

MARGARET FULLER OSSOLI
to an Unknown Person

*After an extended stay in Italy writer and editor Margaret Fuller Ossoli (1810–1850) boarded the **Elizabeth** for passage back to America. With her was her husband, the Marquis Giovanni Angelo Ossoli, and their infant son, Angelino. At 3:30 A.M. on the morning of July 19, 1840, the **Elizabeth** struck a sandbar off Fire Island. The passengers were thrown out of their bunks, as the blow drove a cargo of marble through the ship's side, flooding the hold. As the ship was not far from land, some of the passengers jumped into the water, the surf carrying them to shore. But those who remained, including Margaret and her family, could not see them reach safety. When Margaret saw her friend Horace Sumner drown when he tried to swim to the beach, she became frightened. She realized her young child would have no chance at all. Others tried to persuade her to leave her son behind, but she refused, maintaining hope that the boat would soon be rescued. A wave broke over the vessel and carried everyone on board to their deaths. Before embarking on the voyage that was to end so tragically, Margaret wrote two bizarrely prescient letters. It is not known to whom the first is addressed. The second is to her mother.*

I am absurdly fearful, and various omens have combined to give me a dark feeling. I am . . . indeed a miserable coward, for the sake of Angelino. I fear heat and cold, fear the voyage, fear biting poverty. I hope I shall not be forced to be brave for him, as I have been for myself and that, if I succeed to rear him, he will be neither a weak nor a bad man. But I love him too much! In case of mishap, however, I shall perish with my husband and my child, and we may be transferred to some happier state. . . . I feel perfectly willing to stay my three-score years and ten, if it be thought I need so much tuition on this planet; but it seems to me that my future upon earth will soon close. It may be terribly trying, but it will not be so very long now. God will transplant the root, if he wills to rear it into fruit-bearing. . . .

I have a vague expectation of some crisis,—I know not what. But it has long seemed, that, in the year 1850, I should stand on a plateau in the ascent of life, where I should be allowed to pause for a while, and take more clear and commanding views than ever before. Yet my life proceeds as regularly as the fates of a Greek tragedy, and I can but accept the pages as they turn.

MARGARET FULLER OSSOLI
to Her Mother

May 14, 1850

I will believe, I shall be welcome with my treasures—my husband and child. For me, I long so much to see you! Should anything hinder our meeting upon earth, think of your daughter, as one who always wished, at least, to do her duty, and who always cherished you, according as her mind opened to discover excellence.

Give dear love, too, to my brothers; and first to my eldest, faithful friend! Eugene; a sister's love to Ellen; love to my kind and good aunts, and to my dear cousin E., God bless them!

I hope we shall be able to pass some time together yet, in this world. But, if God decrees otherwise, here and HEREAFTER, my dearest mother,

Your loving child,
Margaret

ALFRED, LORD TENNYSON
to Robert Monteith

Alfred, Lord Tennyson (1809–1892) revealed his interest in poetry at an early age and amazingly by the time he was fourteen years old he had composed a 6,000-line epic poem. Tennyson went on to become one of the best-known and most prolific poets of his time. He is most remembered for "In Memoriam," the poem written in honor of his best friend, Arthur Hallam, who died at the age of twenty-two. Owing to his extreme short-sightedness, Tennyson had difficulty writing and reading and composed much of his poetry in his head. In 1851 Tennyson mourned the loss of a still-born child. He wrote of this experience to his friend Robert Monteith, with whom he had been a member of The Apostles, an undergraduate philosophical club at Cambridge University.

April 24, 1851

My dear Robert,

I am quite sure you feel with me. My poor little boy got strangled in being born. I would not send the notice of my misfortune to the *Times* and I have had to write some 60 letters. If you desire to know about it ask Edmund Lushington to show you that letter which I wrote to him. My wife has been going on very well since; but last night she lost her voice and I thought I should lose her: she is however free from all danger this morning according to my medical man. I have suffered more than ever I thought I could have done for a child still-born: I fancy I should not have cared so much if he had been a seven months spindling, but he was the grandest-looking child I had ever seen. Pardon my saying this. I do not speak only as a father but as an Artist—if you do not despise the word from German associations. I mean as a man who has eyes and can judge from seeing.

I refused to see the little body at first, fearing to find some pallid abortion which would have haunted me all my life—but he looked (if it be not absurd to call a newborn babe so) even majestic in his mysterious silence after all the turmoil of the night before.

He was—not born, I cannot call it born for he never breathed—but he was released from the prison where he moved for nine months on Easter Sunday. Awful day! We live close upon an English-church chapel. The organ rolled—the psalm sounded—and the wail of a woman in her travail—of a true and tender nature suffering, as it seemed intolerable wrong, rose ever and anon.

. . . God bless you and your wife, dear Robert,

For ever and ever,
A. Tennyson

WILLIAM WORDSWORTH
to Robert Southey

In June 1812, poet William Wordsworth (1770–1850) learned that his not-yet-four-year-old daughter, Catherine, had died. Neither parent was with the child at her death or funeral as both were visiting friends far from home. On December 1 of that same year, their son, six-year-old Thomas, succumbed to pneumonia after a serious bout of the measles. He was buried beside his sister in the graveyard across the road from their home. This constant reminder of her two dead children was too much for Wordsworth's wife, Mary, and they moved soon after. Outwardly Wordsworth retained self-control but inwardly he was suffering terribly. To his friend Robert Southey, he confessed his feelings. Southey had given Wordsworth great comfort when his brother, John, died.

December 2, 1812
Wednesday Evening

My dear Friend,

Symptoms of the measles appeared upon my Son Thomas last Thursday; he was most favorable held till Tuesday . . . ; without any assignable cause a sudden change took place, an inflammation had commenced on the lungs which it was impossible to check and the sweet Innocent yielded up his soul to God before six in the evening. He did not appear to suffer much in body, but I fear something in mind as he was of an age to have thought much upon death, a subject to which his mind was daily led by the grave of his Sister.

My Wife bears the loss of her Child with striking fortitude. . . . For myself dear Southey I dare not say in what state of mind I am; I loved the Boy with the utmost love of which my soul is capable, and he is taken from me—yet in the agony of my spirit in surrendering such a treasure I feel a thousand times richer than if I had never possessed it. God comfort and save you and

all our friends and us all from a repetition of such trials—O
Southey feel for me! . . . Best love from everybody—you will
impart this sad news to your Wife. . . .

Heaven bless you

Your sincere Friend
W. Wordsworth

Will Mrs. Coleridge please to walk up to the Calverts and
mention these afflictive news with the particulars. I should have
written but my sorrow over-powers me.

WOLFGANG AMADEUS MOZART
to Abbé Bullinger

*Austrian musician and composer Wolfgang Amadeus Mozart (1756–
1791) was admired and held in awe for his prodigious talents. He composed keyboard pieces, oratorios, symphonies, and operas, producing
such works as* **Don Giovanni** *and* **The Magic Flute.** *In 1778, when
his mother, Anna Maria, died while traveling with him, Mozart acted
with fortitude and discretion. Afraid of the effect his mother's death
would have on his father, Mozart called upon the family's confidential
friend, the Abbé Bullinger, to assist in gently and gradually telling his
father of her passing.*

Paris, July 3, 1778

My dear Friend,

Sympathise with me on this the most wretched and melancholy day of my life. I write at two o'clock in the morning to
inform you that my mother—my dearest mother—is no more!
God has called her to himself. I saw clearly that nothing could
save her, and resigned myself entirely to the will of God; he
gave, and he can take away. Picture to yourself the state of
alarm, care and anxiety in which I have been kept for the last
fortnight. She died without being conscious of anything—her
life went out like a taper. Three days ago she confessed, received the sacrament and extreme unction; but since that time
she has been constantly delirious and rambling, until this afternoon at twenty-one minutes after five, when she was seized
with convulsions, and immediately lost all perception and feeling. I pressed her hand and spoke to her; but she neither saw
me, heard me, nor seemed in the least sensible; and in this state
she lay for five hours, namely, till twenty-one minutes past ten,
when she departed, no one being present but myself, M. Haine,
a good friend of ours whom my father knows, and the nurse.

I cannot at present write you the whole particulars of the illness; but my belief is that she was to die—that it was the will of God. Let me now beg the friendly service of you, to prepare my poor father by gentle degrees for the melancholy tidings. I wrote to him by the same post, but told him no more than that she was very ill, and now I await his answer, by which I shall be guided. May God support and strengthen him! Oh my friend! through the especial grace of God I have been enabled to endure the whole with fortitude and resignation, and have long since been consoled under this great loss. In her extremity I prayed for two things: a blessed dying hour for my mother, and courage and strength for myself; and the gracious God heard my prayer, and richly bestowed those blessings upon me. Pray therefore, dear friend, support my father. Say what you can to him in order that when he knows the worst he may not feel it too bitterly. I commend my sister also to you from the bottom of my heart. Call on both of them soon, but say no word of the death—only prepare them. You can do and say what you will; but let me be so far at ease as to have no new misfortune to expect. Comfort my dear father and my dear sister, and pray send me a speedy answer. Adieu. I remain,

Your much obliged and grateful servant,
Wolfgang Amadeus Mozart

ALPHONSE DE LAMARTINE
to Count Raigecourt

Alphonse de Lamartine (1790–1869) was a French statesman, poet, and historian. His reputation as a polished orator was well known; his speeches strongly influenced government officials as well as public opinion, often swaying extremist views. A leader of the revolution of 1848, Lamartine became the chief of the French provisional government but fell from power with the coup d'état of Napoleon III. He retired from politics and devoted his life to writing. A talented romantic poet, he was credited with revitalizing lyric poetry in France. He wrote this letter of sympathy to Count Raigecourt, a family friend, on the death of Raigecourt's mother.

March 21, 1832

My dear Raoul,

The blow which you have sustained has struck me forcibly too. You know that, when you were still only a child, I was already like a son for your wonderful mother and she acted towards me and guided me as she would have done for you. I have never found in any woman such kindly, sustained and motherly feelings towards me. I had become accustomed to considering her as the earliest member of that type of honorary family which kindred feeling and gratitude create for us when we are solitary wanderers in the world, far from the wings of our real family. So her loss leaves in my thoughts and heart, as also in the happy pattern of my Parisian days, a gap which can never be filled. I am reaching the time of life when these gaps are multiplied daily to detach us little by little from a world where only regrets are bound to be durable.

Although you are so young, you have already experienced many sore trials: your strong spirit will be further fortified by them. But this moral strength which suffering gives us by tempering us in its flames cannot alas equal that straightforward and tender affection which we bring into this world and which ought to be enjoyed longer with objects worthy of love. All the same you have still much left to love: a wonderful father, children whom I hear are delightful, and sisters, one of whom will take the place of a mother for you, if need be, and for your children. Her heart, devoted entirely to others, has kept back for itself only pity for everyone. How overwhelmed she must be!

I was greatly touched by the kindness of Madame de Lascases, who informed me so speedily of the sad event. I see she understood that no one would be more affected by it nor have the sad right to share in it sooner and more completely. Thank her again from me.

I shall visit you probably two months from now, before leaving for Constantinople. It will be a sad and painful occasion for me.

Keep a bit of your mother's tenderness for me, all of you. It is my portion of her inheritance and I shall never renounce it.

Lamartine

RAF PILOT
to His Mother

We know very little about the anonymous author of this farewell letter except that it was written during the Second World War by a young pilot who was part of a Royal Air Force bomber squadron.

Dearest Mother,

Though I feel no premonition at all, events are moving rapidly, and I have instructed that this letter be forwarded to you should I fail to return from one of the raids which we shall shortly be called upon to undertake. You must hope on for a month, but at the end of that time you must accept the fact that I have handed my task over to the extremely capable hands of my comrades of the Royal Air Force, as so many splendid fellows have already done.

First, it will comfort you to know that my role in this war has been of the greatest importance. Our patrols far out over the North Sea have helped to keep the trade routes clear for our convoys and supply ships, and on one occasion our information was instrumental in saving the lives of the men in a crippled lighthouse relief ship. Though it will be difficult for you, you will disappoint me if you do not at least try to accept the facts dispassionately, for I shall have done my duty to the utmost of my ability. No man can do more, and no one calling himself a man could do less.

I have always admired your amazing courage in the face of continual setbacks; in the way you have given me as good an education and background as anyone in the country; and always kept up appearances without ever losing faith in the future. My death would not mean that your struggle has been in vain. Far from it. It means that your sacrifice is as great as mine. Those who serve England must expect nothing from her; we debase ourselves if we regard our country as merely a place in which to eat and sleep.

History resounds with illustrious names who have given all, yet their sacrifice has resulted in the British empire, where there is a measure of peace, justice, and freedom for all, and where a higher standard of civilization has evolved, and is still evolving, than anywhere else. . . . For all that can be said against it, I still maintain that this war is a very good thing; every individual is having the chance to give and dare all for his principles like the martyrs of old. However long the time may be, one thing can never be altered—I shall have lived and died an Englishman. Nothing else matters one jot nor can anything ever change it.

You must not grieve for me, for if you really believe in religion and all that it entails that would be hypocrisy. I have no fear of death; only a queer elation. . . . I would have it no other way. The universe is so vast and so ageless that the life of one man can only be justified by the measure of his sacrifice. We are sent to this world to acquire a personality and a character to take with us that which can never be taken from us. . . .

I count myself fortunate in that I have seen the whole country and known men of every calling. But with the final test of war I consider my character fully developed.

CATHERINE OF ARAGON
to King Henry VIII

Catherine of Aragon (1485–1536) was widowed at the early age of eighteen. Her parents then promised her to twelve-year-old Henry VIII. When Henry acceded to the throne of England six years later, the couple celebrated their marriage. They had one child, Mary, but Henry was obsessed with having a male heir and was convinced that God was showing his displeasure over the union by refusing them a son. Henry publicly demanded an annulment but the Pope refused. Determined, Henry declared himself to be the Head of the Church of England and granted himself an annulment. He became cruel and vindictive, disallowing Catherine even to see Mary. Henry, as we all know, went on to have five more wives, two of whom he beheaded; his second, Anne Boleyn, was accused of adultery and found guilty of high treason. Many thought she was executed because their first and only surviving child was female. Despite his behavior, Catherine remained devoted to Henry until her death and declared her undying love and loyalty to him in her final letter.

1535

My Lord and Dear Husband,

I commend me unto you. The hour of my death draweth fast on, and my case being such, the tender love I owe you forceth me, with a few words, to put you in remembrance of the health and safeguard of your soul, which you ought to prefer before all worldly matters, and before the care and tendering of your own body, for that which you have cast me into many miseries and yourself into many cares.

For my part I do pardon you all, yea, I do wish and devoutly pray God that He will also pardon you.

For the rest I commend unto you Mary, our daughter, beseeching you to be a good father unto her, as I heretofore desired. I entreat you also, on behalf of my maids, to give them marriage-portions, which is not much, they being but three. For all my other servants, I solicit a year's pay more than their due, lest they should be unprovided for.

Lastly, do I vow, that mine eyes desire you above all things.

SIR WALTER RALEGH
to Elizabeth Ralegh

*Sir Walter Ralegh (1552–1618) was an explorer, poet, and historian. He was a favorite of Queen Elizabeth I, supposedly having endeared himself to her by spreading his cloak across a puddle so she could walk over it. Queen Elizabeth appointed him Captain of the Guard, and after his adventures took him to the New World, she knighted him and made him Lord and Governor of Virginia. His name is marked today with the city of Raleigh, North Carolina. However, when the queen heard of his love affair with one of her maids of honor, Elizabeth Throckmorton, she had him thrown into the Tower of London. Once released, Ralegh married his Besse but was soon confined to the Tower again by James I, who framed him as a conspirator in a plot against the crown. While imprisoned he wrote his **History of the World**. Thinking he was to be executed the next day, Ralegh wrote this letter to his wife. However, he was once again released, only to be rearrested and eventually executed in 1618.*

December 1603

You shall now receive my dear wife my last words in these my last lines. My love I send you that you may keep it when I am dead, and my counsel that you may remember it when I am no more. I would not by my will present you with sorrows, dear Besse, let them go to the grave with me and be buried in the dust. And seeing that it is not God's will that I should see you any more in this life, bear it patiently, and with a heart like thy self.

First, I send you all the thanks which my heart can conceive or my words can rehearse for your many travails and care taken for me, which though they have not taken effect as you wished, yet my debt to you is not the less: but pay it I never shall in this world.

Secondly, I beseech you for the love you bear me living, do not hide your self many days, but by your travails seek to help your miserable fortunes and the right of your poor child. Thy mourning cannot avail me, I am but dust.

Thirdly, you shall understand, that my land was conveyed *bona fide* to my child; the writings were drawn at midsummer. . . . And I trust my blood will quench their malice that have cruelly murdered me: and that they will not seek also to kill thee and thine with extreme poverty.

To what friend to direct thee I know not, for all mine have left me in the true time of trial. And I perceive that my death was determined from the first day. Most sorry I am God knows that being thus surprised with death I can leave you in no better estate. . . . Love God, and begin to repose your self upon him, and therein shall you find true and lasting riches, and endless comfort. . . .

Teach your son also to love and fear God while he is yet young, that the fear of God may grow with him, and then God will be a husband to you, and a father to him; a husband and a father which cannot be taken from you.

. . . When I am gone, no doubt, you shall be sought for by many, for the world thinks that I was very rich. But take heed of the pretences of men, and their affections, for they last not but in honest and worthy men, and no greater misery can befall you in this life than to become a prey, and afterwards to be despised. I speak not this, God knows, to dissuade you from marriage, for it will be best for you, both in respect of the world and of God. As for me, I am no more yours, nor you mine; death hath cut us asunder, and God hath divided me from the world, and you from me.

. . . God is my witness it was for you and yours that I desired life, but it is true that I disdained my self for begging of it: for know it, my dear wife, that your son is the son of a true man, and one who in his own respect despiseth death and all his misshapen and ugly forms.

I cannot write much . . . it is time I should separate my

thoughts from the world . . . I can say no more, time and death call me away.

. . . My dear wife farewell. Bless my poor boy. Pray for me, and let my God hold you both in his arms.

Written with the dying hand of sometime thy Husband, but now alas overthrown.

Yours that was, but now not my own.
Walter Ralegh

III. Elegies

FUNERAL BLUES
W. H Auden

Stop all the clocks, cut off the telephone,
Prevent the dog from barking with a juicy bone,
Silence the pianos, and with muffled drum
Bring out the coffin, let the mourners come.

Let aeroplanes circle moaning overhead
Scribbling on the sky the message He is Dead,
Put crepe bows round the white necks of the public doves,
Let the traffic policemen wear black cotton gloves.

He was my North, my South, my East and West,
My working week and my Sunday rest,
My noon, my midnight, my talk, my song;
I thought love could last for ever; I was wrong.

The stars are not wanted now; put out every one,
Pack up the moon and dismantle the sun,
Pour away the ocean and sweep up the wood;
For nothing now can ever come to any good.

FOOTSTEPS OF ANGELS
Henry Wadsworth Longfellow

When the hours of Day are numbered,
And the voices of the Night
Wake the better soul, that slumbered,
To a holy, calm delight;

Ere the evening lamps are lighted,
And, like the phantoms grim and tall,

Shadows from the fitful firelight
Dance upon the parlor wall;

Then the forms of the departed
Enter at the open door;
The beloved, the true-hearted,
Come to visit me once more;

He, the young and strong, who cherished
Noble longings for the strife,
By the roadside fell and perished,
Weary with the march of life!

They, the holy ones and weakly,
Who the cross of suffering bore,
Folded their pale hands so meekly,
Spake with us on earth no more!

And with them the Being Beauteous,
Who unto my youth was given,
More than all things else to love me,
And is now a saint in heaven.

With a slow and noiseless footstep
Comes that messenger divine,
Takes the vacant chair beside me,
Lays her gentle hand in mine.

And she sits and gazes at me
With those deep and tender eyes,
Like the stars, so still and saint-like,
Looking downward from the skies.

Uttered not, yet comprehended,
Is the spirit's voiceless prayer,
Soft rebukes, in blessings ended,
Breathing from her lips of air.

Oh, though oft depressed and lonely,
All my fears are laid aside,
If I but remember only
Such as these have lived and died!

Death takes us by surprise
And stays our hurrying feet;
The great design unfinished lies,
Our lives are incomplete.

SOMETHING TO REMEMBER ME BY
Inge Auerbacher

In the fall of 1944 Inge Auerbacher was a nine-year-old girl impris-
oned with thousands of others in Terezin, Hitler's holding camp in
Czechoslovakia for Jews before their transfer to Auschwitz, Buchen-
wald, Bergen-Belsen, or other death camps. Mourning the recent depar-
ture of her close friend, Inge walked through a small park near her
barracks. She explained, "A middle-aged man raced up to me. He was
very nervous. He handed me a cardboard box filled with trinkets—
handmade items made of string and odds and ends. He gave it to me as
if he had to give it to somebody, anybody. He said, 'Here's something to
remember me by.' He raced away and never said his name. I had never
seen him before and I never saw him again."

He was a stranger; we had never met.
He wanted me to recall him, not to forget.

He handed me a box filled with treasure
And hoped it would give me much pleasure.
Odds and ends up to the brim,
For dreams of any child's whim.
"Something to remember me by!"

I was startled and full of surprise.
A rainbow of color before my eyes.
Things made of threads attached to eternity,
Knitted by loving hands without identity.

His eyes looked hopeless; in a daze,
He walked restless, as if in a maze.
He was a humble man—without fame,
Staying unknown—never stating his name.
"Something to remember me by!"

He rode away on the death train,
Filled with desperation and pain.
He rests with the ashes in sleep,
His memory I will forever keep.

The little girl, now fully grown,
Remembers him, though still unknown.
To this day his words sound loud and clear,
His presence assured from year to year.
"Something to remember me by!"

IN LOVING MEMORY: E. M. BUTLER
Cecil Day-Lewis

"Goodbye"—the number of times each day one says it!
But the goodbyes that matter we seldom say,
Being elsewhere—preoccupied, on a visit,
Somehow off guard—when the dear friend slips away

Tactfully, for ever. And had we known him
So near departure, would we have shut our eyes
To the leaving look in his? tried to detain him
On the doorstep with bouquets of goodbyes?
I think of one, so constant a life-enhancer

That I can hardly yet imagine her dead;
Who seems, in her Irish courtesy, to answer
Even now the farewell I left unsaid.

Remembering her threefold self—a scholar,
A white witch, a small girl, fused into one—
Though all the love they lit will never recall her,
I warm my heart still at her cordial sun. . . .

ON A DYING BOY
William Bell

Oh leave his body broken on the rocks
where fainting sense may drown beneath the sound
of the complaining surf. His spirit mocks
our ignorant attempts to hem it round:
as eagerly as body sought the ground
into its native ocean must it flow.
Oh let his body lie where it was found,
there's nothing we can do to help him now.

And hide his face under his tattered coat
until the women come to where he lies,
they come to bind the silence in his throat
and shut the eternal darkness in his eyes,
to wash the cold sweat of his agonies
and wash the blood that's clotted on his brow.
Cover his face from the unfriendly skies,
there's nothing we can do to help him now.

And watch even his enemies forget him,
the skies forget his sobs, the rocks his blood:
and think how neither rock nor sky dared let him
grow old enough for evil or for good;
and then forget him too. Even if we could

bring back the flower that's fallen from the bough,
bring back the flower that never left the bud,
there's nothing we can do to help him now.

THE BITTER RIVER
Langston Hughes

Dedicated to the memory of Charlie Lang and Ernest Green, both fourteen years old when they were brutally lynched together beneath the Shubuta Bridge over the Chickasawhay River in Mississippi on October 12, 1942.

There is a bitter river
Flowing through the South.
Too long has the taste of its water
Been in my mouth.
There is a bitter river
Dark with filth and mud.
Too long has its evil poison
Poisoned my blood.

I've drunk of the bitter river
And its gall coats the red of my tongue,
Mixed with the blood of the lynched boys
From its iron bridge hung,
Mixed with the hopes that are drowned there
In the snake-like hiss of its stream
Where I drank of the bitter river
That strangled my dream:
The books studied—but useless,
Tool handled—but unused,
Knowledge acquired but thrown away,
Ambition battered and bruised.
Oh, the water of the bitter river
With your taste of blood and clay,

You reflect no stars by night,
No sun by day.

The bitter river reflects no stars—
It gives back only the glint of steel bars
And dark bitter faces behind steel bars:
The Scottsboro boys behind steel bars,
Lewis Jones behind steel bars,
The voteless share-cropper behind steel bars,
The labor leader behind steel bars,
The soldier thrown from a Jim Crow bus behind steel bars,
The 15¢ mugger behind steel bars,
The girl who sells her body behind steel bars,
And my grandfather's back with its ladder of scars,
Long ago, long ago—the whip and steel bars—
The bitter river reflects no stars.

"Wait, be patient," you say.
"Your folks will have a better day."
But the swirl of the bitter river
Takes your words away.
"Work, education, patience
Will bring a better day."
The swirl of the bitter river
Carries your "patience" away.
"Disrupter! Agitator!
Trouble maker!" you say.
The swirl of the bitter river
Sweeps your lies away.
I did not ask for this river
Nor the taste of its bitter brew.
I was given its water
As a gift from you.
Yours has been the power
To force my back to the wall
And make me drink of the bitter cup
Mixed with blood and gall.

You have lynched my comrades
Where the iron bridge crosses the stream,
Underpaid me for my labor,
And spit in the face of my dream.
You forced me to the bitter river
With the hiss of its snake-like song—
Now your words no longer have meaning—
I have drunk at the river too long:
Dreamer of dreams to be broken,
Builder of hopes to be smashed,
Loser from an empty pocket
Of my meagre cash,
Bitter bearer of burdens
And singer of weary song,
I've drunk at the bitter river
With its filth and its mud too long.

Tired now of the bitter river,
Tired now of the pat on the back,
Tired now of the steel bars
Because my face is black,
I'm tired of segregation,
Tired of filth and mud,
I've drunk of the bitter river
And it's turned to steel in my blood.

Oh, tragic bitter river
Where the lynched boys hung,
The gall of your bitter water
Coats my tongue.
The blood of your bitter water
For me gives back no stars.
I'm tired of the bitter river!
Tired of the bars!

DECEASED
Langston Hughes

Harlem
Sent him home
In a long box—
Too dead
To know why:
The licker
Was lye

SURPRISED BY JOY
William Wordsworth

Surprised by joy—impatient as the Wind
I turned to share the transport—Oh! with whom
But Thee, deep buried in the silent tomb,
That spot which no vicissitude can find?
Love, faithful love, recalled thee to my mind—
But how could I forget thee? Through what power,
Even for the least division of an hour,
have I been so beguiled as to be blind
To my most grievous loss!—That thought's return
Was the worst pang that sorrow ever bore,
Save one, one only, when I stood forlorn,
Knowing my heart's best treasure was no more;
That neither present time, nor year unborn
Could to my sight that heavenly face restore.

DIRGE WITHOUT MUSIC
Edna St. Vincent Millay

I am not resigned to the shutting away of loving hearts in the
    hard ground.
So it is, and so it will be, for so it has been, time out of mind:
Into the darkness they go, the wise and the lovely. Crowned
With lilies and with laurel they go; but I am not resigned.

Lovers and thinkers, into the earth with you.
Be one with the dull, the indiscriminate dust.
A fragment of what you felt, of what you knew,
A formula, a phrase remains—but the best is lost.
The answer quick and keen, the honest look, the laughter,
    the love—
They are gone. They have gone to feed the roses. Elegant
    and curled
Is the blossom. Fragrant is the blossom. I know. But I do not
    approve.
More precious was the light in your eyes than all the roses in
    the world.
Down, down, down into darkness of the grave
Gently they go, the beautiful, the tender, the kind;
Quietly they go, the intelligent, the witty, the brave.
I know. But I did not approve. And I am not resigned.

BLUES (FOR HEDLI ANDERSON)
W. H. Auden

Ladies and gentlemen, sitting here,
Eating and drinking and warming a chair,
Feeling and thinking and drawing your breath,
Who's sitting next to you? It may be Death.

As a high-stepping blondie with eyes of blue
In the subway, on beaches, Death looks at you;
And married or single or young or old,
You'll become a sugar daddy and do as you're told.

Death is a G-man. You may think yourself smart,
But he'll send you to the hot-seat or plug you through the
    heart;
He may be a slow worker, but in the end
He'll get you for the crime of being born, my friend.

Death as a doctor has first-class degrees;
The world is on his panel; he charges no fees;
He listens to your chest, says—"You're breathing. That's
    bad.
But don't worry; we'll soon see to that, my lad."

Death knocks at your door selling real estate,
The value of which will not depreciate;
It's easy, it's convenient, it's old world. You'll sign,
Whatever your income, on the dotted line.

Death as a teacher is simply grand;
The dumbest pupil can understand.
He has only one subject and that is the Tomb;
But no one ever yawns or asks to leave the room.

So whether you're standing broke in the rain,
Or playing poker or drinking champagne,
Death's looking for you, he's already on the way,
So look out for him tomorrow or perhaps today.

I SHALL NOT CRY RETURN
Ellen M. H. Gates

I shall not cry Return! Return!
Nor weep my years away;
But just as long as sunsets burn,
And dawns make no delay,
I shall be lonesome—I shall miss
Your hand, your voice, your smile, your kiss.

Not often shall I speak your name,
For what would strangers care
That once a sudden tempest came
And swept my gardens bare,
And then you passed, and in your place
Stood Silence with her lifted face.

Not always shall this parting be,
For though I travel slow,
I, too, shall claim eternity
And find the way you go,
And so I do my task and wait
The opening of the outer gate.

SONNET 71: NO LONGER MOURN
FOR ME WHEN I AM DEAD
William Shakespeare

No longer mourn for me when I am dead
Than you shall hear the surly sullen bell
Give warning to the world that I am fled
From this vile world with vilest worms to dwell:
Nay if you read this line, remember not,
The hand that writ it, for I love you so

That I in your sweet thoughts would be forgot,
If thinking on me then should make you woe.
Oh, if, I say, you look upon this verse,
When I perhaps compounded am with clay,
Do not so much as my poor name rehearse,
But let your love even with my life decay;
Lest the wise world should look into your moan
And mock you with me after I am gone.

REMEMBRANCE
Emily Jane Brontë

Cold in the earth—and the deep snow piled above thee,
Far, far removed, cold in the dreary grave!
Have I forgot, my only Love, to love thee,
Severed at last by Time's all-severing wave?

Now, when alone, do my thoughts no longer hover
Over the mountains, on that northern shore,
Resting their wings where heath and fern-leaves cover
Thy noble heart for ever, ever more?

Cold in the earth—and fifteen wild Decembers
From those brown hills, have melted into spring:
Faithful, indeed, is the spirit that remembers
After such years of change and suffering!

Sweet Love of youth, forgive, if I forget thee,
While the world's tide is bearing me along;
Other desires and other hopes beset me,
Hopes which obscure, but cannot do thee wrong!

No later light has lightened up my heaven,
No second morn has ever shone for me;
All my life's bliss from thy dear life was given,
All my life's bliss is in the grave with thee.

But when the days of golden dreams had perished,
And even Despair was powerless to destroy;
Then did I learn how existence could be cherished,
Strengthened, and fed, without the aid of joy.

Then did I check the tears of useless passion—
Weaned my young soul from yearning after thine;
Sternly denied its burning wish to hasten
Down to that tomb already more than mine.

And, even yet, I dare not let it languish,
Dare not indulge in memory's rapturous pain;
Once drinking deep of that divinest anguish,
How could I seek the empty world again?

WHEN I AM DEAD, MY DEAREST
Christina Rossetti

When I am dead, my dearest,
Sing no sad songs for me;
Plant thou no roses at my head,
Nor shady cypress tree:
Be the green grass above me
With showers and dewdrops wet;
And if thou wilt, remember,
And if thou wilt, forget.

I shall not see the shadows,
I shall not feel the rain;
I shall not hear the nightingale

Sing on, as if in pain:
And dreaming through the twilight
That doth not rise nor set,
Haply I may remember,
And haply may forget.

REMEMBER
Christina Rossetti

Remember me when I am gone away,
Gone far away into the silent land;
When you can no more hold me by the hand,
Nor I half turn to go, yet turning stay.
Remember me when no more, day by day
You tell me of our future that you planned;
Only remember me; you understand
It will be late to counsel then or pray.
Yet if you should forget me for a while
And afterwards remember, do not grieve;
For if the darkness and corruption leave
A vestige of the thoughts that once I had,
Better by far you should forget and smile
Than that you should remember and be sad.

ON MY FIRST SON
Ben Jonson

Farewell, thou child of my right hand, and joy;
My sin was too much hope of thee, lov'd boy:
Seven years thou wert lent to me, and I thee pay,
Exacted by thy fate, on the just day.
O could I lose all father now! For why
Will man lament the state he should envy,

To have so soon 'scaped world's and flesh's rage,
And, if no other misery, yet age?
Rest in soft peace, and asked, say, "Here doth lie
Ben Jonson his best piece of poetry."
For whose sake henceforth all his vows be such
As what he loves may never like too much.

ANTHEM FOR DOOMED YOUTH
Wilfred Owen

What passing-bells for these who die as cattle?
Only the monstrous anger of the guns.
Only the stuttering rifles' rapid rattle
Can patter out their hasty orisons.
No mockeries for them; no prayers nor bells;
Nor any voice of mourning save the choirs—
The shrill, demented choirs of wailing shells;
And bugles calling for them from sad shires.

What candles may be held to speed them all?
Not in the hands of boys, but in their eyes
Shall shine the holy glimmers of goodbyes.
The pallor of girls' brows shall be their pall;
Their flowers the tenderness of patient minds,
And each slow dusk a drawing-down of blinds.

THEY ARE ALL GONE INTO THE WORLD OF LIGHT
Henry Vaughan

They are all gone into the world of light!
And I alone sit ling'ring here;
Their very memory is fair and bright,
And my sad thoughts doth clear.

It glows and glitters in my cloudy breast,
Like stars upon some gloomy grove,
Or those faint beams in which this hill is drest,
After the sun's remove.

I see them walking in an air of glory,
Whose light doth trample on my days:
My days, which are at best but dull and hoary,
Mere glimmering and decays. . . .

HERACLITUS
William Johnson Cory

They told me, Heraclitus, they told me you were dead,
They brought me bitter news to hear and bitter tears to shed.
I wept as I remember'd how often you and I
Had tired the sun with talking and sent him down the sky.
And now that thou art lying, my dear old Carian guest,
A handful of gray ashes, long, long ago at rest,
Still are thy pleasant voices, thy nightingales, awake;
For Death, he taketh all away, but them he cannot take.

L'ENVOI
James Michener

My ship is set to sail to seas unknown
The bo's'n calls my name and I must go.
The bird to guide us on our way has flown
Enticing me to ports I do not know.
Myself when young did eagerly explore
And never stopped till I had reached the moon,
Trod Gobi's sands and heard Zambezi's roar,
Spied Bora Bora in her snug lagoon.

I dream of all the glories I have seen
Karnak and Thebes and Angkor, treasures three.
Great Himalayas with their peaks serene
And blood-red Petra steeped in mystery.
The gods who shared such wonders in the past
Have surely saved the very best till last.

THE OLD FAMILIAR FACES
Charles Lamb

I have had playmates, I have had companions,
In my days of childhood, in my joyful school-days—
All, all are gone, the old familiar faces.

I have been laughing, I have been carousing,
Drinking late, sitting late, with my bosom cronies—
All, all are gone, the old familiar faces.

I loved a Love once, fairest among women
Closed are her doors on me, I must not see her—
All, all are gone, the old familiar faces.

I have a friend, a kinder friend has no man.
Like an ingrate, I left my friend abruptly;
Left him, to muse on the old familiar faces.

Ghost-like I paced round the haunts of my childhood.
Earth seemed a desert I was bound to traverse,
Seeking to find the old familiar faces.

Friend of my bosom, thou more than a brother,
Why wert not thou born in my father's dwelling?
So might we talk of the old familiar faces.

How some they have died, and some they have left me,
And some are taken from me; all are departed;
All, all are gone, the old familiar faces.

PRESENCE OF MIND
Harry Graham

When, with my little daughter Blanche,
I climbed the Alps, last summer,
I saw a dreadful avalanche
About to overcome her;
And, as it swept her down the slope,
I vaguely wondered whether
I should be wise to cut the rope
That held us twain together.

I must confess I'm glad I did
But still I miss the child—poor kid!

THE GOING
Thomas Hardy

Why did you give no hint that night
That quickly after the morrow's dawn,
And calmly, as if indifferent quite,
You would close your term here, up and be gone
Where I could not follow
With wing of swallow
To gain one glimpse of you ever anon!

Never to bid good-bye,
Or lip me the softest call,
Or utter a wish for a word, while I

Saw morning harden upon the wall,
Unmoved, unknowing
That your great going
Had place that moment, and altered all.

Why do you make me leave the house
And think for a breath it is you I see
At the end of the alley of bending boughs
Where so often at dusk you used to be;
Till in darkening dankness
The yawning blankness
Of the perspective sickens me!

You were she who abode
By those red-veined rocks far West,
You were the swan-necked one who rode
Along the beetling Beeny Crest,
And, reining nigh me,
Would muse and eye me,
While Life unrolled us its very best.

Why, then, latterly did we not speak,
Did we not think of those days long dead,
And ere your vanishing strive to seek
That time's renewal? We might have said,
"In this bright spring weather
We'll visit together
Those places that once we visited."

Well, well! All's past amend,
Unchangeable. It must go.
I seem but a dead man held on end
To sink down soon . . . O you could not know
That such swift fleeing
No soul forseeing—
Not even I—would undo me so!

ONE ART
Elizabeth Bishop

The art of losing isn't hard to master;
so many things seem filled with the intent
to be lost that their loss is no disaster.

Lose something every day. Accept the fluster
of the lost door keys, the hour badly spent.
The art of losing isn't hard to master.

Then practice losing farther, losing faster:
places, and names, and where it was you meant
to travel. None of these will bring disaster.

I lost my mother's watch. And look! my last, or
next-to-last, of three loved houses went.
The art of losing isn't hard to master.

I lost two cities, lovely ones. And, vaster,
some realms I owned, two rivers, a continent.
I miss them, but it wasn't a disaster.

—Even losing you (the joking voice, a gesture
I love) I shan't have lied. It's evident
the art of losing's not too hard to master
though it may look like (Write it!) like disaster.

SAY NOT, THEY DIE, THOSE SPLENDID SOULS
Anonymous

Say not, they die, those splendid souls
Whose life is winged with purpose fine;
Who leave us, pointed to the goals;
Who learn to conquer and resign.

Such cannot die; they vanquish time,
And fill the world with glowing light,
Making the human life sublime
With memories of their sacred might.

They cannot die whose lives are part
Of the great life that is to be;
Whose hearts beat with the world's great heart,
And throb with its high destiny.

Those souls are great, who, dying, gave
A gift of greater life to man;
Death stands abashed before the brave;
They own a life death cannot ban.

A SLUMBER DID MY SPIRIT SEAL
William Wordsworth

A slumber did my spirit seal;
I had no human fears;
She seemed a thing that could not feel
The touch of earthly years.

No motion has she now, no force;
She neither hears nor sees;
Rolled round in earth's diurnal course,
With rocks, and stones, and trees.

THE TWENTY-THIRD PSALM

The Lord is my shepherd; I shall not want.
He maketh me to lie down in green pastures;
He leadeth me beside the still waters.
He restoreth my soul;
He leadeth me in the paths of righteousness for His Name's
  sake.
Yea, though I walk through the valley of the shadow of death,
I will fear no evil; for Thou art with me;
Thy rod and Thy staff they comfort me.
Thou preparest a table before me in the presence of mine
  enemies;
Thou anointest my head with oil; my cup runneth over.
Surely goodness and mercy shall follow me all the days of my
  life,
And I will dwell in the house of the Lord forever.

LES JARDINS
Jacques Delille

Visit me, then, in my dark retreat,
There where bending branches gently wave
Sweet illusion will show you my ghost
Sitting on my grave.

There sometimes, doleful and desolate,
To beguile me again in my abode of gloom
At the end of a lovely day, you will come to visit
My poetic tomb.

And if ever you should chance to linger
In this place of peace, love, and mourning
And shed a tear or two upon my coffin
From each falling drop would roses spring.

MONODY ON THE DEATH OF FRANCIS JOHNSON
R. Douglass, Jr.

What means this gathering? thousands seem to crowd
With murmuring voices, deep, but yet not loud;
They gaze with eager eyes, and pressing near,
Methinks on many cheek I see a tear.

A tone of sorrow doth the mass pervade,
And grief hath here bestowed her deepest shade;
No one is joyous here—no one seems glad
But the childhood, youth, and age, all, all, are sad. . . .

He who for years, delighted grave and gay,
The great musician, he hath passed away.
On him no more shall gaze a mortal eye,
But on the thoughts he left, which cannot die;

Immortal like the soul, and those who grieve,
Can gather from them much that may relieve.
Who hath not felt his viol's wond'rous power
Unequall'd oft in pleasure's hour; . . .

Who can forget his ever winning smile,
His jovial heart, his life so void of guile,
His ready eagerness to serve a friend,
Which gave a charm that nothing else can lend; . . .

Now in the earth is placed the mortal part
Of him whose harmony entranced each heart,

And music mournfully breathes o'er the dead
The dirge that for a mighty spirit fled,

He had composed. Tears flowed from every eye,
Sorrowing that one so talented should die.
Weep not that death has quenched his living fire,
Johnson we trust has joined the immortal choir!

BECAUSE I COULD NOT STOP FOR DEATH
Emily Dickinson

Because I could not stop for Death,
He kindly stopped for me;
The carriage held but just ourselves
And Immortality.

We slowly drove, he knew no haste,
And I had to put away
My labor, and my leisure too,
For his civility.

We passed the school where children played
Their lessons scarcely done;
We passed the fields of grazing grain,
We passed the setting sun. . . .

NOW I LAY ME DOWN TO SLEEP
Anonymous

Now I lay me down to sleep,
I pray the Lord my soul to keep.
Four corners to my bed,
Four angels there aspread:

Two to foot and two to head,
And four to carry me when I'm dead.
If any danger come to me,
Sweet Jesus Christ, deliver me.
And if I die before I wake,
I pray the Lord my soul to take.

TO MY FRIEND ON THE DEATH OF HIS SISTER
John Greenleaf Whittier

Thine is a grief, the depth of which another
May never know;
Yet, o'er the waters, O my stricken brother!
To thee I go. . . .

I will not mock thee with the poor world's common
And heartless phrase,
Nor wrong the memory of a sainted woman
With idle praise.

With silence only as their benediction,
God's angels come
Where, in the shadow of a great affliction,
The soul sits dumb!

Yet, would I say what thy own heart approveth:
Our Father's will,
Calling to Him the dear one whom He loveth,
Is mercy still.

Not upon thee or thine the solemn angel
Hath evil wrought:
The funeral anthem is a glad evangel,
The good die not!

God calls our loved ones, but we lose not wholly
What He hath given;
They live on earth, in thought and deed, as truly
As in His heaven.

And she is with thee; in thy path of trial
She walketh yet;
Still with the baptism of thy self-denial
Her locks are wet.

Up then, my brother! Lo, the fields of harvest
Lie white in view!
She lives and loves thee, and the God thou servest
To both is true.

WHAT OF THE DARKNESS?
TO THE HAPPY DEAD PEOPLE
Richard Le Gallienne

What of the Darkness? Is it very fair?
Are there great calms? and find we solace there?
Like soft-shut lilies, all your faces glow
With some strange peace our faces never know,
With some strange faith our faces never dare—
Dwells it in Darkness? Do you find it there?

Is it a Bosom where tired heads may lie?
Is it a Mouth to kiss our weeping dry?
Is it a Hand to still the pulse's leap?
Is it a Voice that holds the runes of sleep?
Day shows us not such comfort anywhere—
Dwells it in Darkness? Do you find it there?

Out of the Day's deceiving light we call—
Day that shows man so great, and God so small,

That hides the stars, and magnifies the grass—
O is the Darkness too a lying glass!
Or undistracted, do you find truth there?
What of the Darkness? Is it very fair?

EARLY DEATH
Hartley Coleridge

She passed away like morning dew
Before the sun was high;
So brief her time, she scarcely knew
The meaning of a sigh.

As round the rose its soft perfume,
Sweet love around her floated;
Admired she grew—while mortal doom
Crept on, unfeared, unnoted.

Love was her guardian Angel here,
But Love to Death resigned her;
Though Love was kind, why should we fear
But holy Death is kinder?

IF I SHOULD GO BEFORE THE REST OF YOU
Joyce Grenfell

If I should go before the rest of you
Break not a flower or inscribe a stone,
Nor when I'm gone speak in a Sunday voice
But be the usual selves that I have known.
Weep if you must,
Parting is hell,

But life goes on
So sing as well.

TO MARY
Charles Wolfe

If I had thought thou couldst have died,
I might not weep for thee;
But I forgot, when by thy side,
That thou couldst mortal be:
It never through my mind had passed
The time would e'er be o'er,
And I on thee should look my last,
And thou shouldst smile no more!

And still upon that face I look,
And think 'twill smile again;
And still the thought I will not brook,
That I must look in vain.
But when I speak—thou dost not say
What thou never left'st unsaid;
And now I feel, as well I may,
Sweet Mary, thou art dead!

If thou wouldst stay, e'en as thou art,
All cold and all serene,
I still might press thy silent heart,
And where thy smiles have been.
While e'en thy chill, bleak corse I have,
Thou seemest still mine own;
But there I lay thee in thy grave—
And I am now alone!

I do not think, where'er thou art,
Thou hast forgotten me;

And I, perhaps, may soothe this heart
In thinking, too, of thee;
Yet there was round thee such a dawn
Of light ne'er seen before,
As fancy never could have drawn,
And never can restore!

AND DEATH SHALL HAVE NO DOMINION
Dylan Thomas

And death shall have no dominion.
Dead men naked they shall be one
With the man in the wind and the west moon;
When their bones are picked clean the clean bones gone,
They shall have stars at elbow and foot;
Though they go mad they shall be the sane,
Though they sink through the sea they shall rise again;
Though lovers be lost love shall not;
And death shall have no dominion.

And death shall have no dominion.
Under the windings of the sea
They lying long shall not die windily;
Twisting on racks when sinews give way,
Strapped to a wheel, yet they shall not break;
Faith in their hands shall snap in two
And the unicorn evils run them through;
Split all ends up they shan't crack;
And death shall have no dominion.

And death shall have no dominion.
No more may gulls cry at their ears
Or waves break loud on the seashores;
Where blew a flower may a flower no more
Lift its head to the blows of the rain;

Though they be mad and dead as nails,
Heads of the characters hammer through daisies;
Break in the sun till the sun breaks down,
And death shall have no dominion.

DO NOT STAND AT MY GRAVE AND WEEP
Anonymous

Do not stand at my grave and weep
I am not there, I do not sleep.
I am a thousand winds that blow,
I am the diamond glint on snow.
I am the sunlight on ripened grain,
I am the gentle autumn rain.
When you wake in the morning hush
I am the swift, uplifting rush
Of quiet birds in circling flight,
I am the soft starlight at night,
Do not stand at my grave and weep
I am not there—I do not sleep.

I'M HERE FOR A SHORT VISIT ONLY
Noël Coward

I'm here for a short visit only
And I'd rather be loved than hated.
Eternity may be lonely
When my body's disintegrated
And that which is loosely termed my soul
Goes whizzing off through the infinite
By means of some vague, remote control,
I'd like to think I was missed a bit.

WHEN I HAVE FEARS AS KEATS HAD FEARS
Noël Coward

When I have fears as Keats had fears,
Of the moment I'll cease to be,
I console myself with vanished years
Remembered laughter, remembered tears,
And the peace of the changing sea.

When I feel sad, as Keats felt sad,
That my life is so nearly done,
It gives me comfort to dwell upon
Remembered friends who are dead and gone
And the jokes we had and the fun.

How happy they are I cannot know
But happy am I who loved them so.

DO NOT LAUGH WHEN THE HEARSE GOES BY
Anonymous

Do not laugh when the hearse goes by
For you may be the next to die.
They'll put you in a wooden shirt
And cover you up with rocks and dirt.
The worms crawl in, the worms crawl out,
They're in your ears and out your snout;
They'll bring their friends and their friends' friends too
And what a mess they'll make of you.

SPIRITS OF THE DEAD
Edgar Allan Poe

Thy soul shall find itself alone
'Mid dark thoughts of the gray tombstone—
Not one, of all the crowd, to pry
Into thine hour of secrecy.

Be silent in that solitude,
Which is not loneliness—for then
The spirits of the dead who stood
In life before thee are again
In death around thee—and their will
Shall overshadow thee: be still.

The night—tho' clear—shall frown—
And the stars shall look not down,
From their high thrones in the heaven,
With light like Hope to mortals given—

But their red orbs, without beam,
To thy weariness shall seem
As a burning and a fever
Which would cling to thee for ever.

Now are thoughts thou shalt not banish—
Now are visions ne'er to vanish—
From thy spirit shall they pass
No more—like dewdrop from the grass.

The breeze—the breath of God—is still—
And the mist upon the hill
Shadowy—shadowy—yet unbroken,
Is a symbol and a token—
How it hangs upon the trees,
A mystery of mysteries!

FOR ANNIE
Edgar Allan Poe

Thank Heaven! the crisis—
The danger is past,
And the lingering illness
Is over at last—
And the fever called "Living"
Is conquered at last. . . .
The sickness—the nausea—
The pitiless pain—
Have ceased, with the fever
That maddened my brain—
With the fever called "Living"
That burned in my brain. . . .

GRIEF
Norah Leney

Deep sobs—
that start beneath my heart
and hold my body in a grip that hurts.
The lump that swells inside my throat
brings pain that tries to choke.
Then tears course down my cheeks—
I drop my head in my so empty hands
abandoning myself to deep dark grief
and know that with the passing time
will come relief.
That though the pain may stay
There soon will come a day
When I can say her name and be at peace.

BEREFT
Thomas Hardy

In the black winter morning
No light will be struck near my eyes
While the clock in the stairway is warning
For five, when he used to rise.
    Leave the door unbarred,
    The clock unwound.
    Make my lone bed hard—
    Would 'twere underground!

When the summer dawns clearly,
And the appletree-tops seem alight,
Who will undraw the curtain and cheerly
Call out that the morning is bright?

When I tarry at market
No form will cross Durnover Lea
In the gathering darkness, to hark at
Grey's Bridge for the pit-pat o' me.

When the supper crock's steaming,
And the time is the time of his tread,
I shall sit by the fire and wait dreaming
In a silence as of the dead.
    Leave the door unbarred,
    The clock unwound.
    Make my lone bed hard—
    Would 'twere underground!

ALONG THE ROAD
Robert Browning Hamilton

I walked a mile with Pleasure;
She chattered all the way,
But left me none the wiser
For all she had to say.

I walked a mile with Sorrow
And ne'er a word said she;
But oh, the things I learned from her
When Sorrow walked with me!

THERE IS NO DEATH
Anonymous

There is a plan far greater than the plan you know;
There is a landscape broader than the one you see.
There is a haven where storm-tossed souls may go—
You call it death—we, immortality.

You call it death—this seeming endless sleep;
We call it birth—the soul at last set free.
'Tis hampered not by time or space—you weep.
Why weep at death? 'Tis immortality.

Farewell, dear voyageur—'twill not be long.
Your work is done—now may peace rest with thee.
Your kindly thoughts and deeds—they will live on.
This is not death—'tis immortality.

Farewell, dear voyageur—the river winds and turns;
The cadence of your song wafts near to me,
And now you know the thing that all men learn:
There is no death—there's immortality.

MY LIFE CLOSED TWICE BEFORE ITS CLOSE
Emily Dickinson

My life closed twice before its close—
It yet remains to see
If Immortality unveil
A third event to me

So huge, so hopeless to conceive
As these that twice befell.
Parting is all we know of heaven,
And all we need of hell.

PSALM OF LIFE
Henry Wadsworth Longfellow

Tell me not, in mournful numbers,
Life is but an empty dream!
For the soul is dead that slumbers,
And things are not what they seem.

Life is real! Life is earnest!
And the grave is not its goal;
Dust thou art, to dust returnest,
Was not spoken of the soul.

Not enjoyment, and not sorrow,
Is our destined end or way;

But to act, that each tomorrow
Find us farther than today.

Art is long, and Time is fleeting,
And our hearts, though stout and brave,
Still, like muffled drums, are beating
Funeral marches to the grave.

In the world's broad field of battle,
In the bivouac of Life,
Be not like dumb, driven cattle!
Be a hero in the strife!

Trust no Future, howe'er pleasant!
Let the dead Past bury its dead!
Act—act in the living Present!
Heart within, and God o'erhead!

Lives of great men all remind us
We can make our lives sublime,
And, departing, leave behind us
Footprints on the sands of time.

Footprints, that perhaps another,
Sailing o'er life's solemn main,
A forlorn and shipwrecked brother,
Seeing, shall take heart again.

Let us, then be up and doing,
With a heart for any fate;
Still achieving, still pursuing,
Learn to labor and to wait.

IV. Epitaphs

Sacred to the Memory of Mr.
Jared Bates who Died Aug. the 6th
1800. His Widow aged 24, who mourns as one who can be
comforted lives at 7 Elm Street this village, possesses every
qualification for a good wife.

LADY CATHERINE DYER'S EPITAPH
FOR HER HUSBAND, SIR WILLIAM DYER

My dearest dust, could not thy hasty day
Afford thy drowszy patience leave to stay
One hower longer: so that we might either
Sate up, or gone to bedd together?
But since thy finisht labour hath possest
Thy weary limbs with early rest,
Enjoy it sweetly: and thy widdowe bride
Shall soone repose her by thy slumbring side.
Whose business, now, is only to prepare
My nightly dress, and call to prayre:
Mine eyes wax heavy and ye day growes old.
The dew falls thick, my belovd growes cold.
Draw, draw ye closed curtaynes: and make roome:
My deare, my dearest dust; I come, I come.

Oh! the worm, the rich worm has a noble domain,
For where monarchs are voiceless, I revel and reign:
I delve at my ease and regale where I may;
None dispute the poor earthworm his will or his way;
The high and the bright for my feasting must fall;
Youth, beauty, and manhood, I prey on ye all!

The prince and the peasant, the monarch and slave,
All, all must bow down to the worm in the grave.

———————

William Large
Caught Cold While Hauling Ice
Died January 21, 1882
Age 25 Years

———————

SARAH RANDALL'S EPITAPH FOR HER DAUGHTER JANE AND
HER HUSBAND JOHN, WHO BOTH DIED IN 1803

Thus to the tomb her dearer half consigned
And at his side a tender pledge resigned.
How lonely is the parent widow's fate
At once to mourn her offspring and her mate.
Thy virtue, John, although nameless left here
Shall long be told by Sarah's silent tear.

———————

*Fannie, the Howe family's pet, was buried at the family plot in 1881
with this epitaph:*

Only a dog, do you say, Sir Critic?
Only a dog, but as truth I prize
The truest love I have won in living
Lay in the deeps of her limpid eyes.
Frosts of winter nor heat of summer
Could make her fail if my footsteps led
And memory holds in its treasure casket
The name of my darling who lieth dead.

ABEL EVAN'S EPITAPH ON ARCHITECT SIR JOHN VANBRUGH

Under this stone, Reader, survey
Dead Sir John Vanbrugh's house of clay.
Lie heavy on him, Earth! for he
Laid many heavy loads on thee!

WESTMINSTER ABBEY ORGANIST JOHN PARSONS

Death passing by and hearing Parsons play
Stood much amazed at his depth of skill,
And said, "This artist must with me away,"
For death bereaves us of the better still;
But let the quire, while he keeps time, sing on,
For Parsons rests, his service being done.

DR. HUGH BOULTER (1671–1742)

A poet so eminent for the
accomplishments of his mind,
the purity of his heart and the excellency of his life that
it may be thought superfluous
to specify his titles, recount his virtues,
or even erect a monument to his fame.

*George Saville (1633–1695), Marquis of Halifax, was given this
informal epitaph by an unappreciative colleague:*

A man of very great and ready wit,
full of life, very pleasant,
much turned to satire,
but with relation to the public
he went backward and forward
so many times, changed sides so many times that in
conclusion no one trusted him.

SAMUEL BUTLER (1612–1680) AT
WESTMINSTER ABBEY'S POETS' CORNER

The Poet's Fate is here in Emblem shown:
He asked for Bread and he received a Stone.

T. S. ELIOT (1888–1965) AT
WESTMINSTER ABBEY'S POETS' CORNER

The communication of the dead is tongued with fire beyond
the language of the living.

APHRA BEHN (1640–1689)

Here lies a proof that wit can never be
Defence against mortality.

The pale consumption gave the silent blow.
The stroke was fatal but the effect was slow.
With wasting pain I sorely was oppress'd

Till God was pleas'd by Death to give me rest.
1799, a youth of 18.

———————

O! Death, how sudden was thy stroke,
The nearest Union Thou has broke;
Nor gave me time to take my leave,
Of my dear Parents left to grieve,
The watery wave; which stop'd my breath,
For want of help, soon caus'd my death.

———————

SARA WHEATLEY

Sinners, prepare to meet your Judge, Your God.
His throne approach with faith in Jesus' blood.
Redemption's only price man's ransom paid
Long in affliction's night my soul afraid.
Triumphing in His cross her house of clay
Now cheerful quits for realms of endless day.

———————

Here lyes
Dame Mary Page
Relict of Sir Gregory Page, Bart.
She departed this life
March 4, 1728,
in the 56th year of age.

In 67 months she was tap'dd 66 times. Had taken away 240
gallons of water, without ever repining at her case or ever fearing the operation.

MEDICINE SEEKER JOHN ST. JOHN LONG (1798–1834)

It is the fate of most men to have many enemies, and few friends. This monumental pile is not intended to mark the career but to show how much its inhabitant was respected by those who knew his worth and the benefits derived from his remedial discovery. He is now at rest and far beyond the praises or censures of this world. Stranger, as you respect the receptacle for the dead (as one of many that will rest here), read the name of John St. John Long without comment.

Henry Russell (1812–1900) apparently had an unnatural relationship with his favorite armchair. His monument is carved the shape of one with these words engraved on it:

I love it, I love it, and who shall dare
To chide me for loving this old arm chair.

Praises on tombs are trifles vainly spent:
A man's good name is his best monument.

ELMA STUART

What though thy name by no sad lips be spoken.
And no fond heart shall keep thy memory green.
Thou yet hast left thine own enduring token,
T'is not as though thou ne'er had been.

KARL MARX (1818–1883)

WORKERS OF ALL LANDS UNITE

The moving finger writes, and having writ, moves on. Nor all thy piety nor wit shall lure it back to cancel half a line, nor all thy tears wash out a word of it.

Harry Thornton, concert pianist, chose this quotation from Puccini for his epitaph:

Sweet thou art sleeping cradled on my heart, Safe in God's keeping while I must weep apart.

I think of Heaven as a garden where I shall find again those dear ones who have made my world.

ELLIZABETH CHAPMAN (1752–1789)

Died of a Broken Heart:
five weeks after her father passed away.

JOHN KENSIT

A martyr for the cause of Christ who fell asleep October 8, 1902, age 49, having been struck down by the missile of an assassin in Birkenhead. Raised of God to defend the Protestant faith and the liberties secured at the blessed Reformation, he laboured throughout England for over thirty years.

LANGFORD REED (1889–1954)

There once was a fellow named Reed
Who knew that the world had a need
For limericks and fun
And all hearts he won
Since laughter and joy were his creed.

The laughter and joy will not die
As angels laugh with him on high
While we here on earth
Should cultivate mirth
'Tis better to laugh than to cry.

EDWARD HARRY WILLIAM MEYERSTEIN (1889–1952)

Memoriae sacrum
Ask not who he was!
Transparent was his character as glass.
Words were his love, a verbal grace his aim.
This stone records an unremembered name.

ALFRED JOHN PRIDELL (1903–1942)

The call was so sudden, the shock severe.
We never thought your end was so near.
Only those who have lost you alone can tell
The pain of parting without a farewell.

H. McNAUGHTON-JONES, M.D. (1869–1949)

Through the mist and cloud the race of life is run.
The goal we do not see till it is won.
Unknown the track, our only signposts years,
The past is shrouded in a mist of tears:
The future lies across an unknown waste.
The present seems the past—with such hot haste. . . .

JULIA GOODMAN (1812–1906)

Thank God she is free from pain

THOMAS JEFFERSON (1743–1826)

Here was buried
Thomas Jefferson

Author of the Declaration of American Independence, of the
Statute of Virginia for religious freedom & Father of the University of Virginia

William Shakespeare was buried in a grave at Stratford-on-Avon in England, but many felt that his body should be interred at Westminster Abbey. His self-made epitaph discourages anyone who would attempt to do so.

Good friend, for Jesus' sake forbeare
To digg the dust enclosed heare;
Bleste be the man that spares these stones,
And curst be he that moves my bones.

N. Grigsby, Abraham Lincoln's brother-in-law by marriage to his oldest sister, instructed friends and family to erect a tombstone over his grave with this inscription:

Through this inscription I wish to enter my dying protest against what is called The Democratic Party. I have watched it closely since the days of Jackson, and know that all the misfortunes of our Nation have come to it through this so-called party. Therefore, beware of this party of treason.

Here lies the body of Susan Lowder
Who burst while drinking a Sedlitz Powder,
Called from this world to her heavenly rest.
She should have waited till it effervesced.

The wedding day
decided was,
The wedding wine
provided;

But ere the day did
come along
He'd drunk it up and
died did.
Ah Sidney! Ah Sidney!

So small, so sweet, so soon
Susan Kay Nason
1960–1969
Forever in Our Hearts

---

*French novelist Stendhal, also known as Marie Henri Beyle, was definitely **not** born in Milan. Many think this unusual epitaph, renouncing his citizenship, was inspired by France's cowardly foreign policy under the reign of Louis Philippe.*

Here lies Henri Beyle of Milan . . . I lived, I wrote, I loved.

HILAIRE BELLOC

When I am dead, I hope it may be said, "His sins were scarlet, but his books were read."

GEORGE DU MAURIER (1834–1896)

A little trust that when we die, we reap our sowing, and so—goodbye!

There is a link death can never sever,
Love and memories last forever.

Here lies Jane Smith, wife of Thomas Smith, Marble cutter.
Monuments of the same style, $350.

Six feet of earth make all men of one size.

Ma Dyed Novem 7 Anno 1696

Youth behold and shed a tear,
Fourteen children slumber here.
See their image how they shine
Like flowers of a fruitful vine.

In this sad tomb, you sleep, O my child!
Listen, my only hope, your mother speaks!
Wake up! You never slept this long before.

Weep not, my loved ones, over that mouldering clay
But look up and ever outward, to my spirit, bright as day.
In life we were united in the earthly bonds of love

We will be bound the same in spirit when we meet in heaven
above.
What to thee can be much sweeter than the thought that I am
near
That I stand ready to greet thee, as thou enter this bright
sphere.

JOHN GAY AT WESTMINSTER ABBEY

Life is a jest; and all things show it,
I thought so once; but now I know it.

Here lies the body of Richard Hind,
who was neither ingenious, sober or kind.

H. J. DANIEL'S EPITAPH FOR HIS WIFE

To follow you I'm not content.
How do I know which way you went?

GEORGE GORDON,
LORD BYRON'S EPITAPH ON CASTLEREAGH

Posterity will ne'er survey
a nobler grave than this:
Here lie the bones of Castlereagh:
Stop, traveller, and piss.

All ye who read with little care,
Who walk away and leave me here,
Should not forget that you must die
And be entombed, as well as I.

By me Mortality is taught,
Your days will pass like mine.
Eternity, Amazing Thought,
Hangs on this Thread of Time.

Behold the glass, Improve thy time
For mine is Run and so must thine.
I have found Godliness Great Gain,
So Run till you the Prize Obtain.

Learn this, ye gay,
That life's a transient flower,
Which grows, and fades,
And withers in an hour.

Death's cold embraces you must try,
And leave the world, as well as I.

May God be kind to Elizabeth,
For she was kind to God.

Sleep, Lovely Babe, and take thy rest.
God called thee early because he liked thee best.

Warm southern sun,
shine softly here,
Warm southern wind,
blow lightly here.
Green sod about, lie light,
lie light.
Goodnight, dear Father,
Goodnight, Goodnight.

Here lies a wife
Of two husbands bereft:
Robert on the right,
Richard on the left.

Near this place lie the bodies of
John Hewet and Sarah Drew
an industrious young man and virtuous maiden
of this parish
Contracted in Marriage who being with many others at Harvest work were both in one instant killed by lightning on the
last day of July 1718.

Behold and see,
As you pass by.
Where you are now,
So once was I.
As I am now,
So you shall be.

Prepare for death,
And follow me.

CHRISTINA ROSSETTI

My harvest is done, its promise ended,
Weak and watery sets the sun,
Day and night in one mist are blended,
My harvest is done.

Long while running, how short when run,
Time to eternity has descended,
Timeless eternity has begun.

Was it narrow the way I wended?
Snares and pits was it mine to shun?
The scythe has fallen so long suspended,
My harvest is done.

DANIEL BOONE

Life's labor done, securely laid
In this his last retreat,
Unheeded o'er his silent dust,
The storms of earth shall beat.

ALEXANDER POPE'S EPITAPH FOR JOHN GAY

Of Manners gentle, of Affections mild;
In Wit, a Man in Simplicity a Child;

With native Humour temp'ring virtuous Rage,
Form'd to delight at once and lash the age;
Above Temptation, in a low Estate;
And uncorrupted, ev'n among the Great;
A safe Companion, and an easy Friend,
Unblam'd thro' Life, lamented in thy End.
These are Thy Honours! not that here thy Bust
Is mix'd with Heroes, or with Kings thy dust;
But that the Worthy and the Good shall say,
Striking their pensive bosoms—Here lies GAY!

SAMUEL TAYLOR COLERIDGE

Poet, Philosopher, Theologian.
This truly great and good man rested for the
Last nineteen years of his life
In this Hamlet.
He quitted "the body of this death"
July 25, 1834,
In the sixty second year of his age.
Of his profound learning and discoursive genius
His literary works are an imperishable record.
To his private worth,
His social and Christian virtues,
James and Anne Gillman,
The friends with whom he resided
During the above period, dedicate this tablet.

Under the pressure of a long
And most painful disease,
His disposition was unalterably sweet and angelic.
He was an ever-enduring, ever loving friend:
The gentlest and kindest teacher:
The most engaging home-companion.

"O! framed for calmer times and nobler hearts,
O studious poet, eloquent for truth!
Philosopher! contemning wealth and death,
Yet docile, childlike, full of life and love,"
Here on thy monumental stone thy friends
Inscribe thy worth;
Reader, for the world, mourn!
A light has passed from the earth,
But, for this pious and exalted Christian,
"Rejoice! and again I say unto you rejoice!!"

When sorrow weeps o'er Virtue's sacred dust,
Our tears become us, and our Grief is just;
Such were the tears she shed, who grateful pays
This last tribute of her love and praise.

In memory of Allegra
daughter of G. G. Lord Byron,
who died at Bagnacavallo,
in Italy, April 20th, 1822,
aged five years and three months
"I shall go to her, but she shall not return to me."
2nd Samuel, XXII, 23.

Giovani Cellini, Benvenuto's only son,
Lies here, remov'd by death in tender years.
Ne'er have the Furies with their murderous shears
From Pole to Pole more hopes destroyed in one.

William Butler Yeats (1865–1939)

No marble, no conventional phrase;
On limestone quarried near the spot
By his command these words are cut:
Cast a cold eye
On life, on death.
Horseman, pass by!

Franz Schubert

The art of music here entombed a rich possession but even
fairer hopes

Sir Arthur Sullivan

Is life a boon?
If so, it must befall
That Death, whene'er he call
Must call too soon!

Captain Robert Falcon Scott and his companions

"To strive, to seek, to win, and not to yield . . ."

Stranger, call this not a place
Of Fear and Gloom.

To me it is a pleasant Spot,
It is my Husband's tomb.

DR. POTTER, ARCHBISHOP OF CANTERBURY, A.D. 1736

Alack and well a-day
Potter himself is turned to clay.

SIR HENRY WOTTON

Here lies the author of this sentence:
An itching for dispute is the scab of the church.
Seek his name elsewhere

Here I lie and no wonder I'm dead
For the wheel of the wagon went over my head

Here lies one MORE, and no More than he.
One More and no More! how can that be?
Why one More and no More may well be here alone
But here lies one More, and that's More than one.

Poorly lived and
poorly died
Poorly buried
And no one cried.

Here lies my wife.
Here let her lie!
Now she's at rest
And so am I.

Here lies a poor woman
Who always was tired,
For she lived in a house
Where help was not hired.

Her last words on earth were:
"Dear friends, I am going
Where washing ain't done,
nor sweeping, nor sewing!

"And everything there
Is exact to my wishes:
For where they don't eat,
There's no washing dishes.

"I'll be where loud anthems
Will always be ringing,
But, having no voice,
I'll get clear o' the singing.

"Don't mourn for me now—
Don't mourn for me never—
I'm going to do nothing
Forever and ever!"

If I am so quickly done for
What on earth was I begun for?

Here lies one Wood
Enclosed in Wood
One Wood within another.
One of these Woods,
Is very good
We cannot praise the other.

Some have children
Some have none
Here lies the mother of twenty-one.

Sacred to the memory of Anthony Drake,
Who died for peace and quietness sake;
His wife was constantly scolding and scoffin',
So he sought for repose in a twelve-dollar coffin.

Owen Moore is gone away
Owin' more than he could pay.

Thus are commemorated the many
multitudes who during the Great
War of 1914–1918 gave the most that

man can give, life itself.
For God
For King and Country
For Loved Ones Home and Empire
For the Sacred Cause of Justice and
The Freedom of the World.

———————

Of children in all she bore twenty-four:
Thank the Lord there will be no more.

———————

Here lyes MARY the Wife of JOHN FORD,
We hope her soul is gone to the LORD;
But if for Hell she has chang'd this life,
She had better be there than be John Ford's wife.

———————

Here a Pretty baby lyes
Sung asleep with lullabies
Pray be silent and not stir
The earth that covers her.

———————

Happy Infant early bless'd
Rest in peaceful slumber rest
Early rescu'd from the cares
Which increase with growing years

STEPHEN REMNANT

Here's a Remnant of life, and a Remnant of death,
Taken off both at once in a remnant of breath;
To mortality this gives a happy release,
For what was the Remnant proves now the whole piece.

Let no one stand behind my grave,
Now that I am called to rest,
Nor shed a tear that I am gone,
For what I need is rest.

Rest from the weary load of care,
Rest from the wearing pain:
For Death shall ever be to me
An everlasting gain.

I know the road was bright and fair
Or once it seemed to be.
But it has changed so much of late,
It has few charms for me.

Here lie I at the Chancel door
Here lie I because I'm poor
The further in the more you'll pay
Here lie I as warm as they.

Best of sons, fondest of husbands,
Paragon of fathers, may you hear our words!
Your family, friends, and subordinates

Will carry their devotion to the grave.
They weep along with us, they water your dust,
But, alas! our tears will not disturb your rest,
Believe, dear Bagnard, in our cruel pain.
Your dying breath lives in our hearts again.

I never cared for Life: Life cared for me:
And hence I owed it some fidelity.
It now says, "Cease; at length thou hast learnt to grind
Sufficient toll for an unwilling mind,
And I dismiss thee—not without regard
That thou didst ask no ill-advised reward,
Nor sought in me much more than thou couldst find."

In memory of the old fish Under the soil
The old fish do lie 20 year he lived and then did die. He was
so tame you understand He would come and eat of your
    hand.
Died April the 20th, 1855

Here lie my husbands One Two Three
Dumb as men could ever be
As for my fourth well praise be God
He bides a little above the sod
Alex Ben Sandy were the
First three names
And to make things tidy
I'll add his—James

Bless my eyes,
Here he lies,
In a sad pickle
Kill'd by an icicle

Here lies Sir Tact, a diplomatic fellow whose silence was not golden but just yellow.

This Egyptian boy of twelve, who refused to have a traditional Egyptian funeral, died of tuberculosis.

I am the son of Epimachus.
Do not pass by my tomb with indifference.
You will not be disturbed by the unpleasant odour of cedar oil.
Listen a while to the words of a dead man who smells good.
Death came to me through a cough, and I passed away as all men must.
So do not weep, my friend, I loathe tears.
It was for this reason that I asked my cousin, Philermes, to refrain from lamentation at my funeral.
Do not inter me in order to disinter me.
Bury me only once, without cedar oil.
The long funeral ceremonies, the women wailing, give me no pleasure.
For every man is destined to die.

Farewell dear wife must we now part
The will of God it must be done

Then for me do not sorrow take
But love my children for my sake.

———————

To these, whom Death again did wed,
This grave's their second marriage-bed
For though the hand of fate could force
'Twixt soul and body a divorce,
It could not sunder man and wife,
'Cause they both lived but one life.
Peace, good Reader. Do not weep.
Peace, the lovers are asleep.

———————

Good people who pass this way,
To God unceasingly please pray
For the soul of the body that lies below.
He was a man of great piety.
Bouchard du Ru was his name.
He died in 1387
On the twenty-fifth day of October.
Pray God he be remembered. Amen!

———————

A lovely young lady I mourn in my rhymes;
She was pleasant, good-natured, and civil sometimes.
And her figure was good: she had very fine eyes,
And her talk was a mixture of foolish and wise.
Her adorers were many, and one of them said,
"She waltzed rather well! It's a pity she's dead!"

ACKNOWLEDGMENTS

THINKING ABOUT AND compiling a book on death and loss can be a lonely pursuit. I was fortunate to have many encouraging people by my side. I would like to thank Sonny and Gita Mehta for their help and hospitality. I am especially indebted to LuAnn Walther for seeing the merit in this project and letting me bring it to fruition as I wished. Her faith in me, advice, and fine company will not soon be forgotten. Much appreciation to Dan Frank for the opportunity to be associated with the integrity and intellectual strength of Pantheon Books. Many thanks are also due to Diana Secker Larson, Ruth Ben-Artzi, and to Lisa Morse, who so many years ago compelled me to reflect on the impact of loss. Special acknowledgment to my parents, Judith and Frank Greenberg, the irreplaceable core.

PERMISSIONS

Chaim Gross. Reprinted by permission of the Renee and Chaim Gross Foundation.

Charles Gwathmey: Eulogy for Robert Gwathmey by Charles Gwathmey. Reprinted by permission of Charles Gwathmey.

Estate of Mother Clara M. Hale: Eulogy for Mother Clara M. Hale by Reverend James A. Forbes. Reprinted by permission of the Estate of Mother Clara M. Hale.

Harcourt Brace & Company: "Ithaka" from *The Complete Poems of Cavafy* by Rae Dalven. Copyright © 1961 and renewed 1989 by Rae Dalven. Reprinted by permission of Harcourt Brace & Company.

Harcourt Brace & Company and HarperCollins Publishers Ltd: Excerpt from *Letters of C. S. Lewis* by C. S. Lewis. Copyright © 1966 by W. H. Lewis and the Executors of C. S. Lewis. Copyright renewed 1994 by C. S. Lewis PTE Ltd. Rights outside the United States administered by HarperCollins Publishers Ltd, London. Reprinted by permission of Harcourt Brace & Company and HarperCollins Publishers Ltd.

Harcourt Brace & Company and The Hogarth Press: Excerpt from *Virginia Woolf: A Biography* by Quentin Bell. Copyright © 1972 by Quentin Bell. Rights outside the United States from THE LETTERS OF VIRGINIA WOOLF administered by The Hogarth Press, a division of Random House UK Ltd, London, on behalf of the Virginia Woolf Estate. Reprinted by permission of Harcourt Brace & Company and the Hogarth Press.

HarperCollins Publishers Ltd.: Excerpt from *The Englishman's Religion* by A. Sampson. Reprinted by permission of HarperCollins Publishers Ltd., London.

HarperCollins Publishers, Inc., and Suhrkamp Verlag: Two letters (May 26, 1949 and March 17, 1950) from *The Hesse/Mann Letters: Correspondence of Hermann Hesse and Thomas Mann*, edited by Anni Carlsson and Volker Michels, and translated by Ralph Manheim. English translation copyright (c) 1975 by Harper & Row, Publishers, Inc. Originally published in German by Suhrkamp Verlag KG. Copyright © 1986 by Suhrkamp Verlag, Frankfurt am Main. Reprinted by permission of HarperCollins Publishers, Inc., and Suhrkamp Verlag.

Sir Rupert Hart-Davis: Eulogy for T. S. Eliot by Sir Rupert Hart-Davis. Reprinted by permission of Sir Rupert Hart-Davis.

Harvard University Press: Excerpt from *The Letters of Henry Wadsworth Longfellow*, Vol. IV (1972). Letter of April 24, 1851, from *The*